Northern Tuscany

Rebecca Ford

D1570287

Credits

Footprint credits
Editor: Nicola Gibbs and Jo Williams
Production and layout: Emma Bryers
Maps: Kevin Feeney
Cover: Pepi Bluck

Publisher: Patrick Dawson
Managing Editor: Felicity Laughton
Advertising: Elizabeth Taylor
Sales and marketing: Kirsty Holmes

Photography credits
Front cover: Bart_J/Shutterstock.com
Back cover: Topora/Shutterstock.com

Printed in Great Britain by CPI Antony Rowe,
Chippenham, Wiltshire

MIX
Paper from
responsible sources
FSC® C013604
www.fsc.org

Publishing information
Footprint *Focus Northern Tuscany*
1st edition
© Footprint Handbooks Ltd
June 2013

ISBN: 978 1 909268 08 1
CIP DATA: A catalogue record for this book
is available from the British Library

® Footprint Handbooks and the Footprint
mark are a registered trademark of
Footprint Handbooks Ltd

Published by Footprint
6 Riverside Court
Lower Bristol Road
Bath BA2 3DZ, UK
T +44 (0)1225 469141
F +44 (0)1225 469461
footprinttravelguides.com

Distributed in the USA by Globe Pequot
Press, Guilford, Connecticut

The content of Footprint *Focus Northern
Tuscany* has been extracted from Footprint's
Tuscany travel guide, which was researched
and written by Rebecca Ford.

Contents

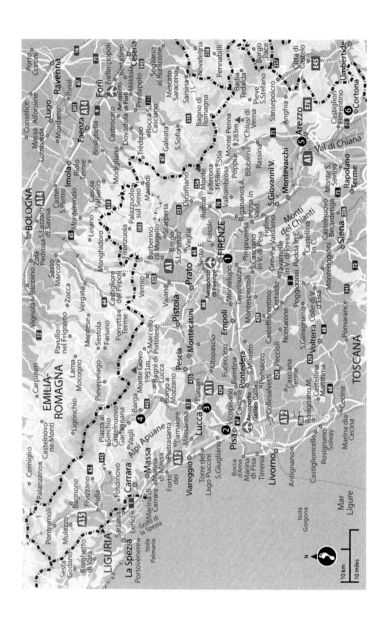

Tuscany is quintessential Italy: a land that launched a thousand picture postcards of rolling hills and vineyards, sunflowers and cypress trees, atmospheric alleyways and historic towns. It's home to the nation's most celebrated city: Florence, the birthplace of the Renaissance, where you can see the world's richest concentration of artistic treasures – and taste some of the finest *gelati*.

Northern Tuscany is wonderfully varied, encompassing top tourist sights as well as remote hills and valleys. Yet many visitors pause here only briefly, beating a path from Pisa airport to the famous Leaning Tower, taking a few photos, buying a cheesy souvenir, then making straight for Florence. But do that and you'll miss so much. Here you'll find one of Tuscany's gems, the medieval city of Lucca, as perfectly preserved inside its medieval walls as an ant entombed in amber. The birthplace of Puccini, it's an easy city to explore on foot or by bike – and a great place to shop for olive oil and regional delicacies.

From Lucca you can drive into the chestnut covered hills of the Garfagnana, a barely explored rural region that's rich in wildlife and laced with walking trails. You can drive into the mountains where marble has been quarried for centuries, buy contemporary works of art in Pietrasanta or dance the night away at coastal resorts like Viareggio – party central in Tuscany. Travel a little further east and you'll find Pistoia. An undeservedly neglected city, squeezed between Lucca and Florence, it has a fine historic centre and a clutch of artistic treasures. Take your time in this region – you'll be rewarded.

In Eastern Tuscany are many works by Piero della Francesca, including his famous fresco cycle in Arezzo, while the medieval hilltop town of Cortona is irresistibly pretty.

Planning your trip

Places to visit in Northern Tuscany

Florence and around
It may be small but Florence is so full of art treasures, Renaissance palaces and fascinating churches that it takes a long time to explore it properly. Michelangelo's *David*, Donatello's St George, Leonardo's *Annunciation*, Ghiberti's Baptistery doors, Fra Angelico's frescoes, Botticelli's *Birth of Venus* – oh, yes, and Brunelleschi's awe-inspiring dome: there's so much to see it can get quite overwhelming. You could spend a weekend in the Uffizi Gallery alone. In high season, the sheer numbers of tour groups – obediently following guides holding umbrellas or sticks aloft like modern-day Pied Pipers – can make it seem as if the city is one big museum. But make time to wander just a short distance from the main sights and you'll be able to see another Florence. Explore the Oltrarno, for example, and you'll find craftsmen producing everything from sculptures to handmade shoes; stroll around Sant'Ambrogio Market and you'll find locals buying fruit and vegetables for that night's dinner. In fact, just get lost in the city and you'll enjoy your trip much more.

Northern Tuscany
Pisa, as Tuscany's main transport hub, is the gateway to much of the region's northern reaches. It sits at the foot of the Monte Pisano, a small mountain range that sets the scene for more dramatic crags further north. The most famous sight is Pisa's Leaning Tower, but the rest of the area offers a good mix of cultural attractions as well as plenty of opportunities for activities. Lucca, birthplace of the composer Puccini, is not just picturesque but extremely musical, staging a wide range of concerts and performances. And each year the Puccini Opera Festival, on the coast at Torre del Lago, attracts thousands of visitors.

In the northwest corner are the mountains where Michelangelo found the marble from which he created his compelling sculptures, and where marble is still quarried today. Here too are the thickly wooded slopes of the Garfagnana, perfect country for a food and wine tour or some exhilarating walks. Further east are: Pistoia, a small city that barely registers on the tourist radar yet has a beautifully preserved centre, the spa town of Montecatini Terme, and Vinci, birthplace of Leonardo.

Eastern Tuscany
While it is more industrialized than other parts of the region, eastern Tuscany also contains the wild Casentino with its forests and crags. The area is certainly not short of attractions. In fact it offers art lovers a real treat, for it's here that you'll find the majority of works by Piero della Francesca – from the *Legend of the True Cross* fresco cycle in Arezzo's San Francesco Church, to the depiction of the pregnant Virgin, the *Madonna del Parto*, in the tiny village of Monterchi. Both Monterchi and Sansepolcro, where the artist was born, are on the border with Umbria but still proudly Tuscan in their outlook. Here you'll also find Cortona, the archetypal Tuscan hill town.

Getting to Northern Tuscany

Air

From UK and Ireland Pisa is the main gateway to Tuscany, and regular flights depart variously from London Gatwick, Heathrow and Stansted, East Midlands, Leeds and Liverpool, with carriers **easyJet**, **Ryanair**, **British Airways** and **Jet2**. While it may be slightly less convenient to fly to Rome, it is still an option that many choose. Florence is a growing airport, and currently **Meridiana** fly direct from London Gatwick. Siena's small airport (aeroportosiena.it) serves executive flights. Overland travel via train and coach or car is viable – more so than for southern Italian regions – but will take a leisurely 24 hours (if you're lucky).

From North America There are no direct flights to Pisa or Florence from North America, but **Continental**, **Alitalia** and **Delta** fly direct from New York to Rome Fiumicino. **Delta** also flies from Toronto via New York. Other airlines that fly from North America to Rome include: **British Airways**, **KLM**, **Lufthansa**, **Swiss**, and **United**. It can also be cost effective to fly via London – or another European hub such as Amsterdam, Frankfurt or Paris – and connect to Pisa or Florence. To search for cheaper flights to Europe from the US, try www.europebyair.com (T(1)866-478 1810).

From rest of Europe Pisa is the most accessible airport, with direct flights from most European cities, including Frankfurt, Paris and Amsterdam. There are direct rail links from Paris, Munich, Vienna and Geneva to international Tuscan train stations.

Airport information Pisa International ① *T050-849300, www.pisa-airport.com*, 80 km west of Florence, is the main international gateway to Tuscany. From the airport it's only a 40-m stroll along a covered walkway to the train station, where you can get a train to Pisa Centrale (five minutes) and change here for a train to Florence. The fare costs €7.90 single and the journey takes about an hour. Alternatively, a **Terravision** ① *www.terravision.eu*, bus runs from Pisa Airport to Florence every 90 minutes from 0840-0020 (70 minutes, €10 return).

From **Florence Airport** ① *T055-306 1300, www.aeroporto.firenze.it*, a **Vola in** bus shuttle (every 30 minutes, €4.50) runs to Santa Maria Novella station.

International travellers may choose to travel from Rome. **Rome Fiumicino** ① *T06-65951, www.adr.it*, is the capital's principal airport. The **Leonardo Express** (www.trenitalia.com) rail service connects the airport to the central station, Roma Termini, every 30 minutes from around 0630-2330. It takes 35 minutes and costs €14 (under 12s free).

Rail

You can travel with **Eurostar** ① *www.eurostar.com*, from London to Paris, before joining an overnight sleeper from Paris Bercy to Florence's Campo di Marte station, just northeast of the centre. Book tickets at www.raileurope.com (T08448 484064; search for trains that depart after 1900), or contact **European Rail** ① *T020-7619 1083, www.europeanrail.com*, a specialist rail agency that can also book rail passes that can save you money. They also offer rail holidays in Italy (T020-7619 1080, www.erail.co.uk). From Florence there are good connections from the main station throughout Tuscany using the Italian train network, www.trenitalia.com.

Road

The 1625-km drive from London to Florence, the region's capital, takes 17 hours' driving time. EU nationals taking their own car need an International Insurance Certificate (also known as a Green Card). Those holding a non-EU licence also need to take an International Driving Permit with them. **Autostrade** ① *T840042121 for road conditions; www.autostrade.it*, provides information on motorways in Italy and **Automobile Club Italiana** ① *T06-49981, www.aci.it*, offers general driving information, as well as roadside assistance with English-speaking operators on T116.

Bus/coach **Eurolines** ① *T08717 818178, www.eurolines.co.uk*, operate three services per week from London Victoria to Florence, with a travel time of around 29 hours. Prices start at £95 return. In Florence coaches arrive and depart at piazza Stazione.

Transport in Northern Tuscany

Rail

Italy has an extensive rail network, and it's the best way to get around the country on a city-based trip – faster than domestic flights: Rome to Florence takes approximately one hour 40 minutes and Florence to Venice two hours 45 minutes. Much of Tuscany is well covered by the rail network.

It's worth knowing that there are several different train services running in Italy: air-conditioned and splendid Eurostar Italia, direct and convenient InterCity, and the slower Regional trains. All can be booked online at **Trenitalia** ① *www.trenitalia.com*, where the type of train is indicated with the initials ES, IC or REG. Amica fares are cheaper advance tickets (if you can find one), flexi fare costs more but is – you guessed it – flexible, and standard fare is just that. You can buy one-country InterRail passes (www.raileurope.co.uk) for Italy (also available for those over 25 these days), which can be used for three, four, six or eight days in one month and range from £167-286 for an adult travelling standard class.

In general, it's more convenient to book online or at ticket machines than it is to queue at a large station in high season. When using a service such as Eurostar Italia or InterCity booking is advised, and a surcharge in addition to a pass will often be required; however, there is no surcharge on the Regional train service. On many Italian trains it's possible to travel 'ticketless', meaning you get on the train and quote your booking reference when the conductor comes round.

If you can't access the internet you can book and buy tickets at train stations, at the counter or via ticket machines. Remember that you must validate tickets at the yellow stamping machines before boarding.

Road

Bicycles and scooters The minimum age for renting a scooter or motorbike is 18. Prices for bike hire are around €10-15 for a day and €50 for a week, while scooter hire starts at about €30 for a day and €175 for a week. Ask at tourist offices for details of local bike/scooter hire companies. Lucca is the most cycle-friendly city in Tuscany.

Bus/coach The bus system in Tuscany is quite extensive and more convenient than rail when you're trying to reach smaller towns and villages. Major bus and coach companies are **Cap** ① www.capautolinee.it, **Florentia Bus** ① www.florentiabus.it, **Lazzi** ① www.lazz.it, **SENA** ① www.sena.it, **TRA.IN** ① www.trainspa.it, and **Sita** ① www.sitabus.it.

Car Driving anywhere in Italy is unlikely to be relaxing, as the Italians have their own inimitable approach to the road. Florence and other towns and cities have pedestrianized centres, so cars have to be parked on the outskirts and buses and trains are a far better option. However, a car is certainly the most convenient way of getting around Tuscany – and essential if you want to visit small villages and wineries. The roads in northern mountain regions such as the Garfagnana are generally quiet, but can be extremely winding. Roads in the southern part of Tuscany are generally the quietest, particularly those in the inland Maremma.

Italy has strict laws on drinking and driving: steer clear of alcohol to be safe. The use of mobile telephones while driving is illegal. Other nuances of Italian road law require children under 1.5 m to ride in the back of the car, and the wearing of a reflective jacket if your car breaks down on the carriageway in poor visibility – make sure you've got one. Since July 2007, on-the-spot fines for minor traffic offences have been in operation – typically they range between €150-250. Always get a receipt if you incur a fine.

Speed limits are 130 km per hour (motorway), 110 km per hour (dual carriageway) and 50 km per hour (town); limits are 20 km per hour lower on motorways and dual carriageways when the road is wet. *Autostrade* (motorways) are toll roads, so keep some cash in the car as a backup, even though you can use credit cards on the blue 'viacard' gates.

Be aware that there are restrictions on driving in historic city centres, indicated by signs with the letters ZTL (*zona a traffico limitato*) in black on a yellow background. If you pass these signs, your registration number may be caught and a fine will be winging its way to you. If your hotel is in the centre of town, you may be entitled to an official pass – contact your hotel or car hire company. However, this pass is not universal and allows access to the hotel only.

Car hire You can hire a car at any of Italy's international airports and many domestic airports; there are plenty of rental companies at Pisa airport. You will probably wish to book the car before you arrive in the country, and it's essential to do so for popular destinations and at busy times of year. Check the opening times of the car hire office in advance.

Car hire comparison websites and agents are a good place to start a search for the best deals. Try www.holidayautos.co.uk, www.easycar.com or www.carrentals.co.uk. Several major car hire companies have offices in Florence, including **Avis** ① www.avisautonoleggio.it, **Hertz** ① www.hertz.it, and **Europcar** ① www.europcar.com.

Check what each hire company requires from you. Some companies will ask for an International Driving Licence, alongside your normal driving licence, if the language of your licence is different to that of the country you're renting the car in. Others are content with an EU licence. You'll need to produce a credit card for most companies. If you book ahead, make sure that the named credit card holder is the same as the person renting and driving the car, to avoid any problems. Most companies have a lower age limit of 21 years and require that you've held your licence for at least a year. Many have a young driver surcharge for those under 25. Confirm insurance and any damage waiver charges and keep all your documents with you when you drive.

Where to stay in Northern Tuscany

There is no shortage of accommodation in Tuscany, and the range of places to stay is enormous. You can find anything from a five-star hotel to a room on a farm. There are private rooms in historic residences, family-run bed-and-breakfast establishments (B&Bs), self-catering apartments, campsites and villas in the countryside. What you won't find is anything particularly cheap, as Tuscany is such a popular tourist destination. Luckily this does also mean that the general standard of accommodation is pretty high. Many properties are historic, so you will find many that don't have lifts or easy access – do check this on booking if it could be a problem.

Prices
Both prices and standards will vary depending on the part of the region you're staying in: Chianti is the most expensive place to stay, but does have some of the region's most charming hotels and *agriturismi*. All establishments must display their prices, at reception and in the rooms, though these will usually be the top rates they'd quote.

You should expect to pay from €100-150 per double room in most places for accommodation graded three stars or above – but this can rise considerably, to well over €400 for the most luxurious (five-star) hotels in Chianti. If you want a single room you'll pay a bit more than if you were sharing.

Prices usually include breakfast, but do check this as it's becoming increasingly common – especially in top-of-the-range establishments – to charge separately for breakfast. In high season, especially in agriturismi, you have to book for a minimum of two or three nights even if you are just staying on a bed-and-breakfast basis. Some places, again often agriturismi, insist that you stay on a half-board basis, with an evening meal included in the price.

Self-catering apartments and villas are usually let for a minimum of a week. With these you are likely to be charged for extras like laundry, cleaning services, electricity and so on – check these out when you first book, otherwise you can get an unwelcome surprise at the end of your stay. Serviced apartments, however, should include cleaning costs in their prices.

As you'd expect, prices vary considerably with the season. They're lowest between November to March, highest at times like Easter and July. The coastal resorts are busiest and most expensive in July and August.

Booking
Do book well in advance to secure the accommodation you want in Tuscany. The best *agriturismi* are frequently booked six months in advance, and it's a good idea to try and book this well ahead for hotels or B&Bs too. An increasing number of hotels, particularly the larger ones, don't publish set prices but vary their rates depending on levels of occupancy. More and more bookings are done on the internet, and sometimes you can get better rates that way. It's always worth asking for a special deal if you're going outside peak season.

Always get confirmation of your accommodation in writing – and confirm it again a day or so before you arrive. Also let people know roughly what time you'll be arriving – you don't want your remote B&B to give away your room because they think you're not coming.

Price codes

Where to stay

€€€€ over €300	€€€ €200-300
€€ €100-200	€ under €100

Prices refer to the cost of two people sharing a double room in the high season.

Restaurants

€€€ over €30	€€ €20-30	€ under €20

Prices refer to the average cost of a two-course meal for one person, including drinks and service charge.

If you want a room with a view (and who doesn't in Tuscany) you'll need to pay extra and should specify on booking. It's also worth checking whether your room overlooks a noisy road.

You'll be asked for your passport at reception, as accommodation providers have to register you with the police. You should get it back quickly. Some B&Bs, small hotels and rental rooms don't accept credit cards – so do check this when you book.

Hotels

Hotels are graded on a star system, with one star the lowest grade and five stars the highest. A *pensione*, a term no longer officially used, would generally be described as a one- or two-star hotel. You might well have no private bathroom in lower grade hotels – so check when booking.

While the star system is a good guide, you'll find considerable variations – especially in three-star establishments in different provinces, and even in the same location. The television in your room, for example, might be an old one stuck high on a shelf or a sleek plasma screen model tastefully displayed. Furniture can also vary from antique or reproduction pieces to a strange array of stuff that looks as if it's come from a junk store.

The bedrooms in Italian hotels have a tendency not to live up to the promise of the reception area. If you're booking your accommodation on the internet, you'll generally be able to see photographs of the *camere* (rooms). If you haven't booked in advance and are just turning up off the street, do ask to see some rooms first. And if you turn up and aren't happy with your room, ask if you can have a different one. But don't be aggressive – that won't get you anywhere here.

Checkout times vary from 1000 to 1200. You might be charged for an extra day if you don't check out in time, but if you ask for a late checkout hotels will often oblige with an extra hour or so if they're not busy.

Agriturismi

In some places you could be forgiven for thinking that every farm is an *agriturismo*. The true *agriturismo* is a working farm that grows or makes its own food or wine. You either stay in a converted barn or outbuilding (usually self-catering) or on a B&B basis in the main house. However, the market has grown so much that the term agriturismo now seems to be applied very loosely to any rural property. The best ones offer things like home-grown food, a swimming pool and a relaxed, welcoming atmosphere.

B&Bs/rooms

Staying at a B&B you can expect a room, usually with private bathroom, in a family home or historic property. Then there are *affitticamere*, or rooms to rent, which may also be in private houses or historic buildings. Some are self-catering (they often have a little kitchen), some offer you the option of breakfast. There will be a reception but there won't necessarily be someone there, or on the premises, all the time.

Food and drink in Northern Tuscany

The Italian nickname for Tuscans is *mangiafagioli* ('bean eaters') – a disparaging reference to the region's traditional reliance on beans as a staple foodstuff. There's no doubt this humble ingredient plays a major role in Tuscan cuisine, which is essentially rustic, but don't think this means you won't eat well here. Tuscans take their food as seriously as they take their appearance – more so in fact – and the style of cooking cleverly combines extreme simplicity with great sophistication. Throughout Tuscany you will find dishes based primarily on a few simple, and extremely fresh, ingredients prepared in a way that highlights their respective flavours. Slow cooking is a feature: nothing is rushed and dishes are eaten separately so that you can fully appreciate what you're eating. When you order a plate of beans you get just that, beans; your salad or meat would comprise another course. Seasonal dishes are also a feature – *funghi* (mushrooms) and chestnuts in the autumn, artichokes in early summer, for instance.

A poor man's feast

Traditional Tuscan cuisine is a *cucina povera*, or 'poor man's cuisine' since, until recent years at least, most people survived on whatever they could grow, hunt or gather. That wasn't too difficult given the productiveness of the landscape, with its fertile fields, dense woodlands filled with chestnuts and mushrooms, abundant herbs, and numerous animals like wild boar and rabbits. Nothing ever went to waste, and even today everything, from calves' tongues and brains to tripe and pigs' trotters, is still painstakingly turned into meals. Every Tuscan must know a hundred ways with leftovers. Yet although meat features prominently, Tuscan food is excellent for vegetarians and many dishes are entirely based on vegetables or beans. Look out for delicious *fagioli al fiasco* – beans cooked in a flask (*fiasco*) with olive oil and black pepper – or pasta such as pappardelle with porcini mushrooms. Bear in mind that soups might be made with meat stock, so check when ordering.

Local specialities

While Tuscan cuisine is different from that of other parts of Italy, it also varies throughout the region, and different areas have their own specialities or versions of classic dishes. Viareggio, on the coast, has a special fish soup called *cacciucco*, which is made with several types of fish and seafood (perhaps cuttlefish, red mullet, shrimps, gurnard, octopus or squid) cooked with tomatoes and garlic and served over thick slices of toast. People in the Garfagnana make good use of the sweet chestnuts that grow in the woods, grinding them into flour to make bread or a rich chestnut cake called *castagnaccio*. You'll also find soups made with *farro* (emmer or spelt), an early type of wheat, as it grows well in the fields here. Then there are the various versions of *acquacotta*, a soup whose name literally means 'cooked water'. It's essentially a soup of the Maremma, made with slowly cooked vegetables then served with a freshly poached egg on top. There's not really a set recipe for it, as each town and even each village has its own slightly different version for the dish.

Renaissance dishes

Some of the richer dishes you'll find on menus have their roots in the courts of the Medici and other noble families. There's *cinghiale in dolce e forte*, for instance, which is wild boar in a 'strong and sweet' sauce with chocolate, vinegar, pine nuts, raisins and rosemary – invented by Florentine chefs during the Renaissance, it's the sort of thing you could imagine Henry VIII tucking into. Even some dishes that are usually considered French have Tuscan origins: crêpes, onion soup and béchamel sauce were taken to France by the chefs of Caterina de' Medici when her court moved to France in the 16th century.

Antipasti

A Tuscan meal usually starts with *crostini* (toasted bread topped with something like *fegatini* (liver pâté) and *affettati* (an assortment of cold cuts such as prosciutto and salami). Look out for toppings of *lardo di Colonnata* too: it's seasoned pork fat from the marble-producing area of Colonnata in the Apuan Alps, in northern Tuscany. The fat, taken from the pig's back, is layered with herbs and salt then stored in cool caves for at least six months. However, the favourite starter is simplicity itself: *fettunta*, literally 'greasy slice', consists of toasted bread rubbed with a clove of garlic and topped with olive oil, preferably the freshest available. Local pecorino cheese features on many menus too, as does *bruschetta* – stale bread topped with fresh tomatoes, garlic and oil.

Primi

The first course is *il primo*. Soups are a big deal: hearty, filling and virtually a meal in themselves, such as *zuppa di faro e fagioli* (bean and barley) or a simple bean soup. Many are made with bread. Tuscan bread is unsalted and, as it goes hard after a few days rather than stale or mouldy, poor families used it up in a variety of ways. You'll often see *pappa al pomodoro* (bread in tomato sauce) or *ribollita* (literally 'reboiled') – a bread, bean and vegetable soup. (If you dunk hunks of bread when you're eating it, the locals will think you're mad.) Bread is also used in *panzanella*, a salad made with soaked stale bread and tomatoes.

Pasta is also served as a first course. In Tuscany this is typically penne, long flat pappardelle, or filled ravioli or tortelli – and it is generally served with fresh porcini mushrooms, a simple tomato sauce or a sauce made from wild boar, rabbit or hare.

Secondi

The second course can be fish but is usually meat, generally served grilled or roasted fairly simply or in a sauce made with a robust red wine. Tuscany's most famous meat dish is *bistecca alla fiorentina*, steak grilled rare or medium and usually served for a minimum of two people (who might be advised to get a new mortgage to pay for it). Favourite meats come from Chianina cattle, raised on the flat lands around Cortona, and from Cinta Senese pigs (black pigs with a distinctive white band. You will also see *lepre* (hare), *piccione* (pigeon), *pollo* (chicken), and the ubiquitous *cinghiale* (wild boar). More hardy types could try trippa (tripe) – a traditional Florentine street food. A typical fish is *baccalà* (salt cod), which is often served with tomato sauce.

Vegetables are a strong point, served as *contorni* (side dishes). You'll be able to try everything from spinach to *cavolo nero* (black cabbage). And then there are beans, of course: cannellini, borlotti, the rare *zolfino* (a tiny white bean) and Hannibal Lecter's favourite, *baccelli* (fava beans). They're often served on their own, stewed for hours with tomatoes and fragrant sage leaves.

Dolci

Desserts are usually something simple like fruit, or *cantuccini* (often sold as biscotti overseas) – hard dry biscuits that you dunk into Vin Santo, a sweet wine. You might also see *zuccotto*, a Florentine dessert of cream, almonds and chocolate surrounded by alcohol-soaked sponge fingers. *Cavallucci* (the name means 'little horses' as they were originally destined for those who worked in the stables) are dense, aniseed-flavoured buns studded with candied fruits, while *ricciarelli* are deliciously chewy almond biscuits. The traditional Sienese Christmas cake is *panforte*, a stick-to-your-ribs mix of honey, dried fruits and almonds – you'll also find a version made with cinnamon and nutmeg called *panpepato*. Look for *pan coi santi* too: it's a spicy loaf with dried fruit and nuts that's only made around All Saints' Day (1 November). The traditional Tuscan cheese is pecorino, a sheep's milk cheese traditionally from Pienza. It can be eaten young and pale, when the flavour is delicate, or mature, when it's darker and more flavoursome.

Olive oil

It would be impossible to imagine Tuscan cuisine without olive oil, which is made everywhere from Lucca to the Maremma. In November, during the olive harvest, families race to get their freshly picked olives to the press as fast as possible. The new oil is hailed with celebratory tastings and festivals – and a gift of good olive oil is always much appreciated. The oil should be kept as airtight as possible, in a dark bottle (to protect it from the light) and out of the heat. The highest quality olive oil is referred to as 'extra virgin' – it comes from the first cold pressing of the olives and must have less than 0.8% acid content.

Wine

Wine accompanies most meals, of course. It's been made in Tuscany since Etruscan times and locals take their wines (which are mainly red) very seriously. Variations in terrain, soil and climate in the Tuscan countryside mean that many different types are produced within a relatively small area. Most are made from varieties of Sangiovese grapes and are now highly rated by wine experts; the days when Chianti was valued mainly for its distinctive – wouldn't-it-make-a-good-lamp – raffia-wrapped bottle are long gone.

The government controls and classifies wines through a system that regulates everything from the types of grapes used to the method of production. Categories start with no-nonsense vino da tavola (table wine), followed by IGT (Indicazione Geografica Tipica). Next up the scale are DOC (Denominazione di Origine Controllata) wines and finally DOCG (Denominazione di Origine Controllata e Garantita) – you can easily recognize these as they'll have a small pink tag on the top.

DOCG wines are determined by the grape varieties used, production methods and geographical area. Look out for the famed, and famously pricey, Brunello di Montalcino, Carmignano, Chianti, Chianti Classico, Vino Nobile di Montepulciano and, the only white in the list, Vernaccia di San Gimignano, which was served at royal weddings in Renaissance times. New kids on the block are the Super-Tuscan wines: made from non-indigenous grape varieties such as Merlot and Cabernet, they've been produced to create a new type of Italian wine with wide international appeal, and are now going at higher prices than traditional DOCG wines.

Chianti Classico bottles are usually distinguished by a black cockerel, but Chianti Rufina and Chianti Colli Fiorentini can be just as good – everything depends on the producer. Don't neglect other parts of Tuscany either. The Maremma is an up-and-coming wine (and oil) producing area. Its best-known wine is the red DOC Morellino di Scansano, but there is

The wine of friendship

While you're in Tuscany make sure you try some Vin Santo, a dark, sweet, fortified wine that tastes a bit like sherry. The name means 'holy wine' as it was once used by the priest for Holy Communion – the local joke was that while he was holding it up and making the sign of the cross he was secretly inspecting the quality and hoping the congregation would leave some for him. Today it's generally considered the wine of friendship. Many people still make it at home, and it's often offered to guests. The grapes are dried in a breezy attic room for three months, then pressed and the juice put in a barrel, or *carratello*, which contains the *mama* – the sediment from the last production – to ferment. It's then placed in a loft and left to age with the seasons. It gets no special treatment and is exposed to extremes of temperature – by the time it's ready, a bottle can stay open for months without spoiling.

also a delicate dry white Bianco di Pitigliano and another DOC red, Montecucco, from the area around Grosseto. Essentially though, don't worry too much about labels, just taste a few and make up your own mind.

Practical information
Tuscan towns and cities, particularly Florence, are well served with places to eat – you'll be able to find restaurants as well as *trattorie and osterie*, which are cheaper. Even the smallest village usually has a bar where you can get coffee and a snack. Lunch is generally taken around 1300 and the evening meal not until after 2000. You'll usually pay around €20-30 per person for a couple of courses and a drink – don't forget the dreaded *pane e coperto* (bread and cover charge) and the service charge, which will be added to your bill.

Bars
Bars in Tuscany tend to double as cafés, attracting everyone from office workers popping in for a slug of espresso first thing in the morning to 20-something students out for a few drinks in the evening. The biggest change in recent years has been the fashion for having *aperitivi* early in the evening. Lots of bars now offer a complimentary buffet with their pre-dinnertime drinks: you'll usually pay a set price of perhaps €6-10; then, if you wish, you can often eat as much as you would for a full meal (great if you're travelling on a budget). Aperitifs are generally available from around 1800 to 1930 or 2000, and bars get very lively at these times. Afterwards people will maybe head home or go for a leisurely meal in a restaurant.

You'll also find some pubs in the main cities – these generally have an Aussie, English, Irish or Scottish theme and tend to attract young locals and students.

Clubs
The biggest clubs are on the outskirts of the city centres and – as you'd expect – most are around Florence. Some offer a dinner and dance package. In summer the clubbing scene moves outdoors, and venues can change from year to year.

Concerts and festivals
Major international bands tend to miss out Tuscany on their tours. If they do stop, it will be in Florence. Contemporary Tuscan acts to look out for include Piero Pelu, formerly with Tuscan band Litfiba; rap artist Jovanotti and experimental outfit Miranda and the Creeping

Nobodies. If you want to check out contemporary music/jazz concerts and festivals, the Toscana Music website is worth a look: www.toscanamusiche.it.

There's a wealth of classical music on offer in Tuscany. In Florence, the big event is the **Maggio Musicale Fiorentino**, and there are also plenty of classical concerts in Lucca and of course Torre del Lago, home of the annual **Puccini Festival**.

Festivals in Northern Tuscany

Festivals play an important role in Tuscany. It's a region in which traditions are part of the rhythm of daily life – they're certainly not there just to entertain the tourists. Many of these festivals are related to the church calendar: saints' feast days and Easter, for example. There are also art, film and music festivals – mainly held in the cities. Yet the most important, and distinctive, festivals of all are those that celebrate local food and wine. Too numerous to name, they are held in towns and villages throughout Tuscany – evidence of the close link that still exists between the people and their land.

February
Carnevale, Viareggio, www.viareggio. ilcarnevale.com. Lively carnival dating back to the 19th-century.

April
Scoppio del Carro (Explosion of the Cart) – Florence, Easter Sunday. A cart loaded with fireworks and pulled by oxen is taken in a colourful, costumed procession through the city.

May
Festa Del Grillo (Festival of the Cricket) – Florence, Ascension Day. Crickets are sold in cages, then released for good luck.
Giostra dell'Archidado, Cortona. Medieval crossbow competition.
Maggio Musical Fiorentino (May Music Festival, maggiofiorentino.com), Florence. Major music festival with opera, classical music and ballet.

June
Calcio Storico (Football in Costume, www.calciostorico.it) – Florence. Held on the feast day of Florence's patron, St John the Baptist, this is a football game played in costume.
Estate Fiesolana (Fiesole Summer Festival, www.estatefiesolana.it). General performing arts festival in Fiesole.
Giostra dell'Orso, Pistoia. The Joust of the Bear. involves a costumed parade and a jousting contest between the town's 4 *contrade*.
Gioco del Ponte, Pisa. A sort of 'push of war' – rather than tug of war, in which rival *contrade* push a heavy cart across the Ponte di Mezzo, on the Arno.
Giostra del Saracino, Arezzo www.giostra delsaracino.arezzo.it. Jousting contest in which contestants try to hit an effigy of a Saracen to win the Golden Lance.

July
Puccini Festival, Torre del Lago, T0584 359322, www.puccinifestival.it. Major opera festival, staging Puccini's works outdoors.

August
Barga Jazz Festival, Aug, and Opera Barga. 2 music festivals held in this medieval town in the Garfagnana.
Cortonantiquaria, www.cortonantiquaria.it, Cortona. This is the oldest antique furniture fair in Italy, with large numbers of dealers coming to the little town.
Fish and Chip Festival. Barga's Scottish connections are celebrated with a communal meal of fish and chips, eaten at long tables outside.

Sagra della Bistecca, Cortona. This outdoor food festival is a celebration of the local Valdichiana beef.
Tuscan Sun Festival (Festival del Sole), Cortona. Ticket office open Jul and Aug, www.festivaldelsole.com. A cultural festival, celebrating music, art, literature and food.

September
La Rificolona (Festival of the Lanterns) – Florence. A procession of children carry lanterns to Piazza SS Annunziata.

Palio della Balestra, Sansepolcro. This costumed medieval festival involves a crossbow competition between teams from Sansepolcro and Gubbio.
Settembre Lucchese, Lucca. The Volto Santo (Holy Face) is paraded through the town.

November
Florence Marathon (www.firenze marathon.it) – Florence. Annual race starting at Piazzale Michelangelo and finishing at Piazza Santa Croce.

Buying a property in Tuscany

There's a small farmhouse with a terracotta tiled roof, shutters at the windows and scarlet geraniums tumbling from pots by the door. There's a garden filled with plump tomatoes, flowers and fragrant basil, and perhaps a field with a few olive trees as well. And there's you and your family enjoying dinner al fresco in your own little corner of Tuscany.

It's easy to get carried away with the thought of buying into the Tuscan dream. Of buying a wrecked barn and turning it into a fabulous holiday home, or retiring there to live the good life. And even though the credit crunch has made us all aware that property isn't the fail-safe investment we once thought, Tuscany still exerts a pull on the imagination that can make you throw caution to the winds.

The thing to remember is to take your time, think carefully about what you want and, above all, ensure that you get proper advice.

The property
Tuscan property is not cheap – if you want a bargain then look elsewhere in Italy. The wrecked barns and farms that were bought for a song in Chianti in the 1960s and 1970s have long gone. If you do want to buy in Tuscany then check out areas such as the Garfagnana, the countryside near Volterra and the inland Maremma, where prices aren't as high as in Chianti or hilltowns like Cortona. And while everyone loves the idea of a rural property, perhaps an apartment or small house in a town or village might be a more practical – and cheaper, bet for you. You might also want to think of buying in a recently restored borgo (hamlet), where everything has already been done.

If you do find a property that needs renovation, bear in mind the costs involved – you could pay around €1000 per sq m. There are strict planning laws as well, and you'll have to use original materials (or at least good copies) as far as possible. And can you be on site to supervise the work? Check out the area carefully too, and see what it's like at different times of day. And remember that Tuscany can get very cold in winter.

Getting there
Think about how you're going to use the property. Are you going to live there, or will it be a second home? If it's the latter you must cost in the price of getting there several times a year. And you don't want to be reliant on just one low cost airline. With fuel prices rising, routes could be cut – so make sure you've got back up options.

The purchase

Don't rush into things – use a reputable agent (registered with the local Chamber of Commerce), and ideally both an Italian lawyer and one in your own country. When you see something you like, you'll be asked to sign a reservation contract and pay a 10% deposit. Before the next stage, you should get a survey done by a geometra (a mix of surveyor/ architect). Make sure that you also check out things like boundaries, rights of way etc as well. You'll also need to check that the property was correctly registered, has planning permission, whether there are any outstanding debts or claims.

The next stage is to sign a *compromesso*, or preliminary contract. This binds you into buying the property. You'd be asked to pay a deposit of about a third of the purchase price – and you'll lose it if you later pull out of the deal.

If you need to arrange an Italian mortgage then remember that one is only available to a maximum of 80% of the property price. Loan periods range between 10, 15, 25 and 30 years.

The final stage is the rogito, completion of sale – you'll usually need to be present for this and funds will need to be in place. You'll need to pay in euros so your money transfer should be arranged.

Fees and taxes

Don't forget other costs – agency fees, purchase tax (10% of the value for a second home), notary (lawyer) fees, geometra fees, translation costs – and then annual taxes for refuse, tv licence and the property.

Useful websites

These include www.italianproperty.eu.com, www.tuscanhomes.com, www.keyitaly.com, www.homesinitaly.co.uk and www.casatravella.com.

Getting married in Tuscany

More and more people are drawn to the idea of getting married in Tuscany. You get a romantic wedding location, guests get a few days in the sun and your honeymoon is sorted.

Italian weddings are becoming increasingly easy to arrange, with many agencies specialising in organising everything from the paperwork to the flowers. A lot of hotels, especially those within countryside locations with pretty churches nearby, are geared up for weddings too. They will be able to stage the reception, do the catering and also accommodate all the guests.

Of course bureaucracy makes its presence felt in a Tuscan wedding, just as it does in all aspects of Italian life. So make sure you use a reputable agency which will let you know exactly what paperwork to provide. This varies with your home country, so UK citizens require slightly different paperwork to people from the US, etc. However, in general, you'll at least need to provide your birth certificate, passport and, if one of you has been married before, either a divorce decree or death certificate of former spouse. Paperwork must be in place to be checked in Italy about three days before the service.

Types of ceremony

Think carefully about the type of ceremony you want. If one of you is a Roman Catholic then you can get married in a catholic church, but you'll also need to show that you have permission from your local bishop, proof of attendance at marriage preparation classes and proof of baptism, first communion and confirmation. However if you're divorced that complicates matters more. If you wanted a Protestant, Jewish or other faith wedding, then there would be different requirements.

A civil ceremony is probably your most straightforward option and is legally recognised worldwide. This must take place in the Town Hall and will be carried out in Italian. An interpreter must also be present for non Italian speakers, as well as two witnesses.

Make sure you plan well ahead to allow time to book the venue, arrange catering, flowers and a photographer, accommodation for you and your guests, and of course, time to ensure all the paperwork goes through correctly and on time.

Useful websites

These include www.toscama.com, www.italyweddings.com, www.gettingmarriedin italy.com and www.italianweddingservices.com.

Essentials A-Z

Customs and immigration
UK and EU citizens do not need a visa, but will need a valid passport to enter Italy. A standard tourist visa for those outside the EU is valid for up to 90 days.

Disabled travellers
Italy is a bit behind when it comes to catering for disabled travellers, and access is sometimes very difficult or ill thought out. For more details, before you travel contact an agency such as **Accessible Italy** (www.accessibleitaly.com) or **Society for Accessible Travel & Hospitality** (www.sath.org).

    Florence Tourism (www.firenzeturismo.it) has a section on its website with information for tourists with special needs. Most of the **ATAF** orange buses in Florence are equipped with a flat car deck and a space for a wheelchair. A door-to-door minibus service is available, but you need to make a reservation 2-3 days in advance: contact Mr Formichetti (T055-565 0486, formichetti@ataf.fi.it). The Florence taxi company **So.Co.Ta** (T055-410133, www.socota.it) has a 6-seat van with an electronic platform: you must book 2 days in advance. Free wheelchair rental in Florence is available from **Arciconfraternita della Misericordia** (piazza del Duomo, T055-212222) and **Fratellanza Militare Firenze** (Oltrarno office, via Sant'Agostino 6, T055-26021, www.fratellanzamilitare.com).

Electricity
Italy functions on a 220V mains supply. Plugs are the standard European 2-pin variety.

Emergencies
Ambulance T118, **Fire service** T115, Police T113 (with English-speaking operators), T112 (carabinieri), **Roadside assistance** T116.

Etiquette
Bella figura – projecting a good image – is important to Italians. Take note of public notices about conduct: sitting on steps or eating and drinking in certain historic areas is not allowed. You need to cover your arms and legs to gain admission to many churches – in some cases shorts are not permitted. Punctuality is apparently not mandatory in Italy, so be prepared to wait on occasion.

Families
Whether they're having a traditional beach break or an afternoon in a *gelateria*, families are well accommodated in Italy. Children are well treated, and there's plenty to do besides endless museum visits. The family is highly regarded and *bambini* are indulged. Note that lone parents, or adults accompanying children of a different surname, may sometimes need to produce evidence of guardianship before taking children in or out of the country. Contact your Italian embassy for current details (Italian embassy in London, T020-7312 2200).

Health
Comprehensive travel and medical insurance is strongly recommended. EU citizens should apply for a free European Health Insurance Card (www.ehic.org), which has replaced the E111 form and offers reduced-cost medical treatment. Late-night pharmacies are identified by a green cross; T1100 for addresses of the 3 nearest open pharmacies. The accident and emergency department of a hospital is the *pronto soccorso*. In Florence the main hospital is the Policlinico di Careggi (viale Pieraccini/viale Morgagni 85, T055-794 9644), outside the city centre.

Insurance

Comprehensive travel and medical insurance is strongly recommended for all travel – the EHIC is not a replacement for insurance. You should check any exclusions, and that your policy covers you for all the activities you want to undertake. Keep your insurance documents separately – emailing all the details to yourself is a good way to keep the information safe and accessible. Ensure you have full insurance if hiring a car; you may need an international insurance certificate if you are taking your own car (contact your current insurers).

Money

The Italian currency is the Euro. There are ATMs throughout Italy that accept major credit and debit cards. To change cash or travellers' cheques, look for a *cambio*. Many restaurants, shops, museums and art galleries take major credit cards. Paying directly with debit cards such as Cirrus is less easy in many places, so withdrawing cash from an ATM to pay may be the better option. Keep some cash for toll roads, if you're driving.

Police

There are 5 different police forces in Italy The *carabinieri* are a branch of the army and wear military-style uniforms with a red stripe on their trousers and white sashes. They handle general crime, drug-related crime and public order offences. The *polizia statale* are the national police force and are dressed in blue with a thin purple stripe on their trousers. They are responsible for security on the railways and at airports. The *polizia stradale* handle crime and traffic offences on the motorways and drive blue cars with a white stripe. The *vigili urbani* are local police who wear dark blue (in summer) or black (in winter) uniforms with white hats; they direct traffic and issue parking fines in the cities. The *guardia di finanza* wear grey uniforms with grey flat hats or green berets (depending on rank). They are charged with combating counterfeiting, tax evasion and fraud. In the case of an emergency requiring police attention, dial 113, approach any member of the police or visit a police station.
Florence: borgo Ognissanti 48, T055-24811 (*carabinieri*); via Pietrapiana 50r, T055 203911, emergency number T055-328 3333.
Arezzo: via Filippo Lippi, T057-54001.
Lucca: piazzale San Donato 12a, T0583-442727.
Pisa: via Mario Lalli 1, T050-583511.

Post

The Italian postal service has a not entirely undeserved reputation for unreliability, particularly when handling postcards. Overseas post requires *posta prioritaria* (priority mail) and a postcard stamp costs from €0.60. You can buy *francobolli* (stamps) at post offices and *tabacchi* (look for T signs).
Florence post office: via Pellicceria 3, also at the Uffizi and via Pietrapiana 53.

Safety

Crime rate in Italy is generally low, though petty crime is higher. Female travellers won't experience the same hassles in Tuscany as they do in southern Italy. A good rule of thumb is to avoid stations and dark areas at night – places like SMN station and Cascine Park in Florence, Pisa station and the narrow streets around the market. Take care when travelling: don't flaunt your valuables; take only what money you need and split it up. Beware of scams and con-artists, and don't expect things to go smoothly if you get involved in buying fake goods. Car break-ins are common, so always remove valuables. Take care on public transport, where pick-pockets and bag-cutters operate. Do not make it clear which stop you're getting off at – it gives potential thieves a timeframe to work in.

Telephone

The code for Florence is 055. You need to use the local codes, even when dialling from within the city or region. The prefix for Italy is +39. You no longer need to drop the initial '0' from area codes when calling from abroad. For directory enquiries T12.

Time difference

Italy uses Central European Time, GMT+1.

Tipping

Only in the more expensive restaurants will staff necessarily expect a tip, although everyone will be grateful for one; 10-15% is the norm, and it's increasingly common for service to be included in your bill on top of the cover charge. When you're ordering at the bar a few spare coins may speed service up. Taxis may add on extra costs for luggage, but an additional tip is always appreciated. Rounding up prices always goes down well, especially if it means not having to give change – not a favourite Italian habit.

Contents

Footprint features

Northern Tuscany

Florence

Florence is the jewel in Tuscany's crown. All roads may lead to Rome, but all art lovers head for Florence. It was here that the Renaissance took root, and where the intellectual luminescence it generated, and the new focus it put on humanity, was first felt in both arts and sciences. Wealthy families in Florence, keen to flaunt their riches, commissioned works by exciting new artists and architects. The city became the place to be if you wanted to make your name – and a living – as an artist. Come to Florence today and you'll find works by Michelangelo, Donatello, Leonardo da Vinci, Botticelli and many more. Sights range from the medieval Ponte Vecchio and the magnificent Duomo to the lavish interiors of the Pitti Palace and the quiet simplicity of Santo Spirito.

The trouble is, there's just too much to see, and Florence's small size can tempt you into thinking you can do it all. You can't. The key to an enjoyable trip is to accept that and allow time for non-cultural pleasures too, like lazy lunches and shopping. Planning's important, as you can save hours of queuing by booking tickets in advance. And don't be disappointed if a museum is closed, or a work of art is being restored – there's always something equally amazing nearby.

What to see in Florence in…

…one day

Visit the Duomo, the Baptistery and climb the Campanile. See the Orsanmichele and have lunch, before a tour of the Palazzo Vecchio. Go to the piazza Santa Croce, to admire the exterior of Santa Croce church, followed by a stroll along the Arno to the Ponte Vecchio. There'll be time for window-shopping on via Tornabuoni, a walk through piazza della Repubblica and finally down to the Mercato Nuovo, to rub the nose of the Porcellino to ensure you return to Florence.

…a weekend or more

Go inside Santa Croce church, and visit either the Uffizi or the Accademia. If you go to the Uffizi, cross the Arno to visit Santa Maria del Carmine and picnic in the Boboli Gardens. If you choose the Accademia, you can also visit San Marco, plus the Medici-Riccardi Palace.

Arriving in Florence

Getting there

The main railway station is Santa Maria Novella (Firenze SMN), piazza Santa Maria Novella in the west of the city. Beside it is the main bus station. International coaches leave from Sitabus station, T0861 1991900, www.eurolines.it. Blue SITA ① *T0800-373760, www.fsbusitalia.it*, coaches arrive and depart from the Sita Bus Station, via Santa Caterina da Siena, near the train station. See Transport, page 64.

Getting around

Florence is a small, compact city and it is easy to get around on foot, especially as non-residents have to park in the main car parks, such as that beneath the station, around Porta San Frediano or by piazzale Michelangelo (www.firenzeparcheggi.it). To reach San Miniato al Monte or Fiesole you can hop on bus 13 by Santa Maria Novella.

Orange ATAF electric buses lines C1, C2, C3, D operate in the city centre, and ordinary ATAF buses (T0800 424500, www.ataf.net) serve longer routes. Buy tickets at tabacchi, bars and newsagents and the ATAF booth in SMN station; single trip €1.20 (€2 if bought on the bus) or four tickets for €4.70 – one validated, tickets last 90 minutes; 24-hr ticket €5, three-day ticket €12. A tram system was completed in 2010 (www.gestramvia.it), with one line linking the centre with the suburb of Scandicci 6 km southwest of the city.

Taxis are metered and you will be charged for each piece of luggage. There are plenty of taxis at Santa Maria Novella, and you will also find them by piazza Santa Croce and piazza del Duomo. If you call a taxi or your hotel calls one for you will be charged an extra €2-3.

Tourist information

Tourist Information Office ① *via Cavour 1r, T055-290832/3, www.firenzeturismo.it, Mon-Sat 0830-1830; (closed on Sun and holidays).* There are also offices at: ① *piazza Stazione 4, T055 212245, www.comune.fi.it, Mon-Sat 0830-1900, Sun and holidays 0830-1400,* and ① *Loggia del Bigallo, piazza San Giovanni, T055 288496, bigallo@comune.fi.it, Mon-Sat 0900-1900, Sun and holidays 0900-1400,* and ① *"Amerigo Vespucci" airport, T055-315874, infoaeroporto@firenzeturismo.it, daily 0830-2030.*

Florence

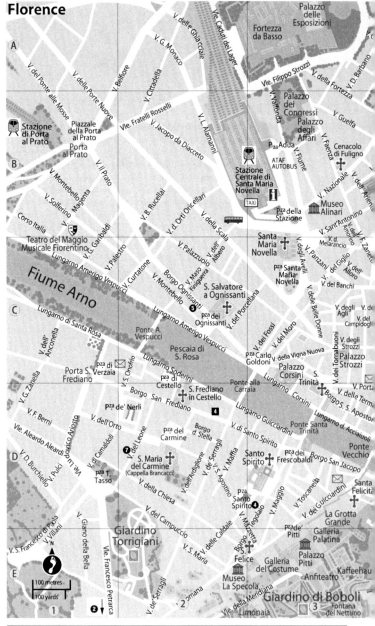

Fortezza
da Basso

Palazzo
delle
Esposizioni

V. delle Ghiacciaie

Vle. Caduti dei Lager

V. G. Monaco

(A)

V. delle Porte Nuove

V. del Ponte alle Mosse

V. Belfiore

V. Cittadella

Vle. Filippo Strozzi

V. della Fortezza

V. D. Barbano

V. C

Stazione
di Porta
al Prato

Piazzale
della Porta
al Prato
Porta
al Prato

Vle. Fratelli Rosselli

V. Jacopo da Diacceto

V. L. Alamanni

Palazzo
dei
Congressi
Palazzo
degli
Affari

P.za Adua

V. Valfonda

V. Fiume

V. Guelfa

V. Faenza

Cenacolo
di Fuligno

(B)

V. Montebello

V. Solferino

Magenta

V. Il Prato

V. B. Rucellai

V. d. Orti Oricellari

V. della Scala

Stazione
Centrale di
Santa Maria
Novella

ATAF
AUTOBUS

TAXI

P.za della
Stazione

V. Nazionale

V. dell'Ariento

Museo
Alinari

P.za della
Stazione

Corso Italia

Teatro del Maggio
Musicale Fiorentino

V. Garibaldi

V. Palestro

V. Palazzuolo

V. Maso Finiguerra

V. dell'
Albero

Santa
Maria
Novella

P.za Santa
Maria
Novella

V. degli Avelli

V. Sant'Antonino

V. d.
Melarancio

V. Panzani

V. del Giglio

V. dell'
Amorino

V. d. Zanetti

V. dell'
Alloro

V. dei Banchi

Fiume Arno

Lungarno Amerigo Vespucci

V. Curtatone

V. Montebello

Borgo Ognissanti

S. Salvatore
a Ognissanti

P.za dei
Ognissanti

V. del Porcellana

5

V. dei Fossi

V. del Moro

V. delle Belle Donne

V. degli
Agli

V. d.
Campidoglio

V. del
Strozzi

V. de' Tornabuoni

(C)

Lungarno di Santa Rosa

V. dell'
Anconella

Ponte A.
Vespucci

Pescaia di
S. Rosa

Lungarno Amerigo Vespucci

Lungarno Soderini

P.za Carlo
Goldoni

V. della Vigna Nuova

Palazzo
Corsini

S.
Trinita

Borgo S. S. Apostoli

Palazzo
Strozzi

V. degli
Strozzi

V. Port

V. delle Term

V. G. Zanella

Porta S.
Frediano

P.za di
Verzaia

V. S. Onofrio

P.za di
Cestello

S. Frediano
in Cestello

Ponte alla
Carraia

Lungarno Corsini

Lungarno d. Acciaiuoli

Ponte
Vecchio

V. F. Berni

Vle. Aleardo Aleardi

V. dell'Orto

Borgo San Frediano

P.za de' Nerli

Borgo
d. Stella

V. di Santo Spirito

Lungarno Guicciardini

Ponte Santa
Trinita

V. d'Ardiglione

(D)

Vle. Ludovico Ariosto

V. Pulci

V. di Camaldoli

V. del Leone

P.za del
Carmine

7

S. Maria
del Carmine
(Cappella Brancacci)

V. de' Serragli

V. S. Agostino

Santo
Spirito

P.za dei
Frescobaldi

Borgo San Jacopo

Santa
Felicita

V. D. Burchiello

P.za T.
Tasso

V. della Chiesa

V. del Campuccio

P.za
Santo
Spirito

4

V. Maggio

V. Mazzetta

V. Toscanella

V. de' Guicciardini

La Grotta
Grande

Galleria
Palatina

Kaffeehau

V. S. Francesco di Paola

V. Villani

Giardino
Torrigiani

Vle. Francesco Petrarca

V. S. Maria

V. delle Caldaie

Borgo Tegolaio

S.
Felice

Galleria
del Costume

P.za de'
Pitti

Palazzo
Pitti

Anfiteatro

(E)

100 metres
100 yards

2

V. de' Serragli

V. Romana

Museo
La Specola

Vle. della Meridiana

Giardino di Boboli

Limonaia

3

Fontana
del Nettuno

1

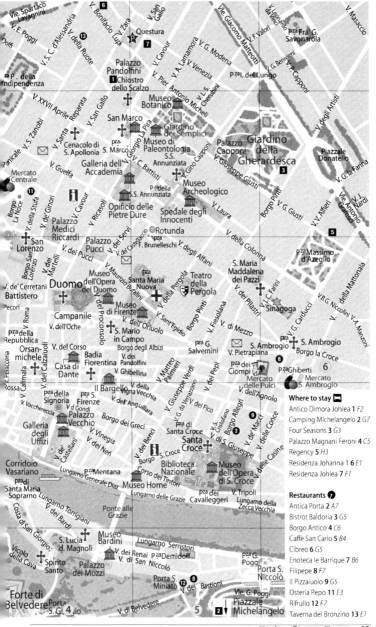

Where to stay 🛏

Antico Dimora Johlea 1 *F2*
Camping Michelangelo 2 *G7*
Four Seasons 3 *G3*
Palazzo Magnani Feroni 4 *C5*
Regency 5 *H3*
Residenza Johanna 1 6 *E1*
Residenza Johlea 7 *F1*

Restaurants ⑦

Antica Porta 2 *A7*
Bistrot Baldoria 3 *G5*
Borgo Antico 4 *C6*
Caffè San Carlo 5 *B4*
Cibreo 6 *G5*
Enoteca le Barrique 7 *B6*
Filipepe 8 *F7*
Il Pizzaiuolo 9 *G5*
Osteria Pepo 11 *E3*
Rifrullo 12 *F7*
Taverna del Bronzino 13 *E1*

Around piazza del Duomo → *For listings, see pages 53-64.*

The piazza del Duomo is surely everyone's first stop in Florence – even if you've been several times before it's hard to resist the pull. Many of the city's top sights are crammed into the piazza; the Duomo itself – topped with Brunellschi's famous dome, the Baptistery, the Bell Tower and the Museo dell'Opera del Duomo. And just a couple of minutes' walk away there's the Orsanmichele, its walls lined with famous statues.

Duomo

ⓘ *Piazza del Duomo, T055-230 2885/215380, www.operaduomofirenze.it, Mon-Wed and Fri 1000-1700, Thu and 1st Sat in month 1000-1530, Sat 1000-1645, Sun 1330-1645, free; crypt (Santa Reparata) €3; cupola Mon-Fri 0830-1900, Sat 0830-1740, €8, combined ticket for cupola with Museo dell'Opera del Duomo €11; entry at porta della Mandorla, north side of cathedral; combined ticket for all the Duomo's attractions €23, valid for 4 days.*

There was a church on this site in the fifth or sixth century – you can see the remains of it in the crypt. However, once the Baptistery was completed in the 13th century, the existing cathedral looked "very crude" in contrast and "small in comparison to so great a city", according to a contemporary writer. Even worse, rival cities such as Pisa and Siena already had magnificent cathedrals that outshone Florence's crumbling version. So the foundation stone of a new cathedral, dedicated to Santa Maria del Fiore (Our Lady of the Flower), was laid in 1296, with Arnolfo di Cambio as the architect. The plan was to create the largest church in Christendom. Arnolfo died early in the 14th century, and the work was completed by other architects. By 1418 all that was lacking was the dome, but the design of the building required this to be so large that no one had any idea how to build it.

Brunelleschi's Dome Furious at losing the commission for creating the Baptistery doors to Lorenzo Ghiberti in 1403, Filippo Brunelleschi had decided to abandon his career as a goldsmith and specialize in architecture instead. He studied works by ancient classical masters and travelled to Rome with his friend Donatello to inspect mighty buildings such as the Pantheon. When a competition was launched to find someone capable of building the cathedral dome, Brunelleschi entered and won. He originally had to work with Ghiberti, who was by now very famous, but downed tools when Ghiberti got the credit for his work. Ghiberti proved unequal to the task and Brunelleschi was eventually able to continue alone.

He managed the seemingly impossible. His octagonal dome is a masterpiece of Renaissance engineering – for a start it was built without scaffolding, with innovative hoists carrying both workers and bricks to the top. The bricks were set in self-supporting patterns, and an inner shell was constructed to support the larger outer shell, making a double dome. Around four million bricks were used, and the structure was finished by 1436.

You can go right up into the dome, which is the best way of appreciating Brunelleschi's astonishing achievement and seeing the stained glass windows and frescoes. The views from the top are stunning, but be warned: there are 463 steps.

Cathedral interior The cathedral was not entirely completed until the 19th century, when the lavish façade was added, using white, red and green marble from Carrara, the Maremma and Prato respectively. After the excesses of the façade, the interior is surprisingly restrained and uncluttered. Perhaps the most striking sight as you enter is that of the two equestrian portraits – on the left Niccolò da Tolentino and on the right the Englishman Sir

Top sights in Florence

The Duomo Brunelleschi's architectural wonder.
Uffizi Gallery Masterpieces galore.
Baptistery Ghiberti's gleaming bronze doors.
Santa Croce Monumental memorials.
San Marco Fra Angelico's moving *Annunciation*.

Palazzo Vecchio Francesco's secret studio.
The Accademia Michelangelo's republican *David*.
The Bargello Donatello's daintier *David*.
Palazzo Medici-Riccardi The Chapel of the Magi.
The Brancacci Chapel Masaccio's *Expulsion from Eden*.

John Hawkwood. Hawkwood was a *condottiere*, or mercenary commander, who fought on behalf of Florence and was promised the honour of an equestrian statue after his death. Instead he got this rather cheaper fresco, painted in 1436 by Paolo Uccello, who utilized the newly acquired knowledge of perspective to create something that looked like a statue. The portrait of Tolentino, by Andrea del Castagno, was done later and has far more life and vigour. There is more of Uccello's work above the main entrance – a **liturgical clock** that tells the time starting each day from the previous sunset, just as the church calculates the timing of religious festivals. The inside of the dome is covered in brilliantly coloured frescoes of the *Last Judgement* (1572-1579), painted by Giorgio Vasari and Federico Zuccari.

If you go downstairs to the **crypt** you can see the remains of the ancient basilica of Santa Reparata, which this cathedral replaced. Archaeological excavations here have revealed that four churches lie beneath the Duomo, with remains dating from the early Christian period. Peep through the metal grille beside the gift shop and you can see the inscription on the tomb of Brunelleschi. It translates as "The body of a man of Great Genius".

Campanile
ⓘ *Daily 0830-1930, €6, combined ticket with Battistero, crypt and Museo dell'Opera del Duomo €15.*
The Bell Tower was started in 1334 by Giotto, but he died before he could finish it. It was completed by Andrea Pisano and later, Francesco Talenti – who had to reinforce the walls to prevent it falling over. The tower stands around 85 m high and offers great views. There are 414 steps to the top.

Battistero di San Giovanni
ⓘ *Mon-Sat 1215-1900, Sun and 1st Sat in month 0830-1400, €3, combined ticket with Campanile, crypt and Museo dell'Opera del Duomo €15.*
For a long time it was supposed that the octagonal Baptistery was originally a Roman temple dedicated to Mars, converted to Christian use. However, most evidence suggests it dates from the sixth century – which still makes it the oldest building in the city. It was here that the poet Dante was baptised. The building was enlarged and reconstructed in the 11th and 12th centuries, and in the 13th century the ceiling was decorated with glorious Byzantine-style mosaics – the main figure is *Christ in Judgment*. The marble floor, also 13th-century, is decorated with signs of the zodiac. A large octagonal font once stood in the centre.

However, it is the **doors of the Baptistery** that are its most famous feature. When one of the city's powerful guilds, the Arte di Calimala, decided that the exterior required embellishment, they engaged Andrea Pisano to create a set of bronze doors (1330-1336)

Central Florence

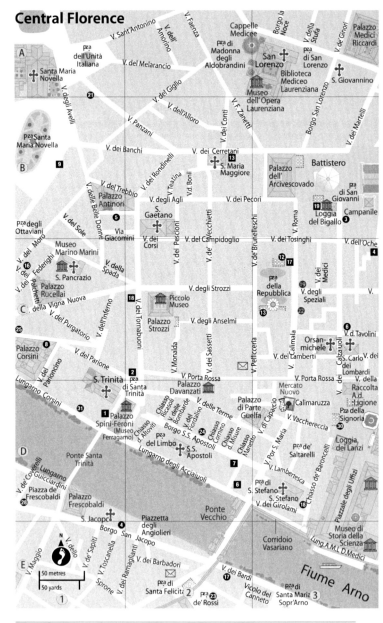

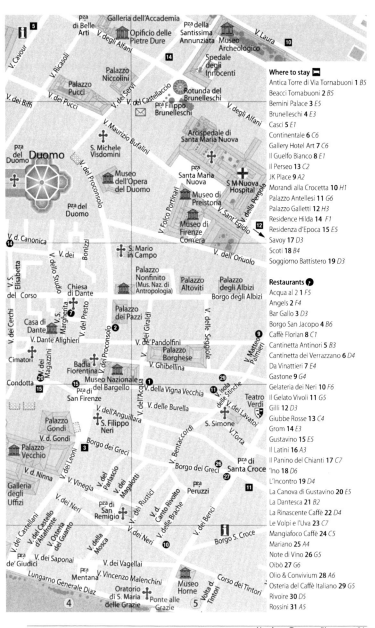

Where to stay 🛏

Antica Torre di Via Tornabuoni 1 *B5*
Beacci Tornabuoni 2 *B5*
Bernini Palace 3 *E5*
Brunelleschi 4 *E3*
Casci 5 *E1*
Continentale 6 *C6*
Gallery Hotel Art 7 *C6*
Il Guelfo Bianco 8 *E1*
Il Perseo 13 *C2*
JK Place 9 *A2*
Morandi alla Crocetta 10 *H1*
Palazzo Antellesi 11 *G6*
Palazzo Galletti 12 *H3*
Residence Hilda 14 *F1*
Residenza d'Epoca 15 *E5*
Savoy 17 *D3*
Scoti 18 *B4*
Soggiorno Battistero 19 *D3*

Restaurants 🍴

Acqua al 2 1 *F5*
Angels 2 *F4*
Bar Gallo 3 *D3*
Borgo San Jacopo 4 *B6*
Caffè Florian 8 *C1*
Cantinetta Antinori 5 *B3*
Cantinetta dei Verrazzano 6 *D4*
Da Vinattieri 7 *E4*
Gastone 9 *G4*
Gelateria dei Neri 10 *F6*
Il Gelato Vivoli 11 *G5*
Gilli 12 *D3*
Giubbe Rosse 13 *C4*
Grom 14 *E3*
Gustavino 15 *E5*
Il Latini 16 *A3*
Il Panino del Chianti 17 *C7*
'Ino 18 *D6*
L'Incontro 19 *D4*
La Canova di Gustavino 20 *E5*
La Dantesca 21 *B2*
La Rinascente Caffè 22 *D4*
Le Volpi e l'Uva 23 *C7*
Mangiafoco Caffè 24 *C5*
Mariano 25 *A4*
Note di Vino 26 *G5*
Oibò 27 *G6*
Olio & Convivium 28 *A6*
Osteria del Caffè Italiano 29 *G5*
Rivoire 30 *D5*
Rossini 31 *A5*

"Balls, Balls, Balls!"

Throughout Florence and Tuscany you'll see a distinctive coat of arms, studded with six large balls or pills (*palle*). This was the emblem of the Medici family. The number of balls varied over the years – in Cosimo's time there were seven, for instance. One theory has it that the balls refer to the family's origins as doctors or apothecaries (*medici*), another that they are coins. The colours have faded today, but the shield was originally gold and the balls red, except for the one at the top, which was blue and decorated with a fleur-de-lys. In times of danger, supporters of the Medici rallied followers with a distinctive call to arms: "*Palle, Palle, Palle!*" – or "Balls, Balls, Balls!" The ubiquity of this distinctive emblem attracted contemporary criticism: "He has emblazoned even the monks' privies with his balls," said one.

containing 28 relief panels depicting scenes in the life of Saint John the Baptist. These are the **south doors**.

In 1401 the Calimala held a competition to design another set of doors – a competition in which Brunelleschi was famously beaten by Ghiberti (you can see their competition pieces in the Bargello, see page 39). The doors essentially became Ghiberti's life's work. The first set, the **north doors** (1403-1424) have 28 relief panels, most depicting scenes from the New Testament. When these were finished, Ghiberti was commissioned to make another set, the now famous **east doors** (1425-1450). The doors you see today are copies (the originals are in the Museo dell'Opera del Duomo, see below) but they're still an impressive sight. There are ten panels of Old Testament scenes, ranging from Adam and Eve being expelled from the Garden of Eden to Moses receiving the Ten Commandments. Ghiberti employed perspective techniques to great effect, filling the panels with drama and vitality. They were dubbed the **Gates of Paradise**, reputedly by Michelangelo, and are often said to represent the 'official' birth of the Renaissance.

Look at the equally elaborate door frames. Roughly in the middle, on the left-hand door, there's the head of a bald man looking rather pleased with himself; beside him, on the right-hand door, is the head of a younger man. They're Ghiberti and his son Vittorio.

Museo dell'Opera del Duomo

ⓘ *Piazza del Duomo 9, T055-230 2885, www.operaduomo.firenze.it, Mon-Sat 0900-1930, Sun 0900-1345, €6, combined ticket with cupola €11; combined ticket with Campanile, crypt and Baptistery €15; combined ticket with Campanile, Baptistery, crypt and cupola €23.*
This museum is devoted to conserving the most precious works, such as statues, associated with the Duomo, the Baptistery and the Campanile. On the ground floor, for example, there are works from the first façade of the cathedral (which was pulled down in the 16th century) including a glassy-eyed Madonna by the first architect, Arnolfo di Cambio. You can also see Ghiberti's original **Gates of Paradise** from the Baptistery.

On the stairs is Michelangelo's *Florentine Pietà*, one of his last works and the sculpture that he wanted on his tomb. He famously became frustrated by it and smashed Christ's arm with a hammer – it was later repaired by an assistant. According to Vasari, the figure of Nicodemus is a self-portrait.

Upstairs you can find many works by Donatello, created for the façade of the Campanile. Most famous is the *Prophet Habbakuk*, which the artist found so realistic that he is said to have grabbed it shouting: "Speak! Speak!" In another room pride of place goes to another

Top Renaissance sights in Florence

Michelangelo's *David* – Accademia.
Donatello's *David* – Bargello.
Masaccio's *Trinity* – Santa Maria Novella –
and his frescoes in the Brancacci Chapel.
Fra Angelico's *Annunciation* – San Marco.

Botticelli's *Primavera* and *Birth of Venus* – Uffizi.
Leonardo's *Annunciation* – Uffizi.
Brunelleschi's *Dome* – Duomo.

work by Donatello, the desperately ravaged figure of *Mary Magdalene* carved in wood. Other treasures in the museum include the death mask of Brunelleschi and the silver altar that was made for the Baptistery.

Orsanmichele
ⓘ *Via dell'Arte della Lana, T055-284944, Tue-Sun 1000-1700, may open until 1930 on Sat in summer, free.*
A short walk from the Duomo, down via dei Calzaiuoli, brings you to the Orsanmichele. If it doesn't look like a church, that's because originally it wasn't one. A ninth-century church once stood here, but it was replaced by a market. However, the place was obviously still imbued with spiritual energy, because a painting of the Madonna on a pillar in the market was soon credited with performing miracles. The first market building burned down and was replaced by the present structure around 1337. It was built specifically to combine commerce and devotion, with the grain market downstairs and the upper floors for religious services. If you look carefully you can still see the grain chutes. The miraculous Madonna was replaced by Bernardo Daddi's painting of the *Madonna delle Grazie* (1346), which was credited with miraculously curing cases of the plague of 1348. The painting is surrounded by an extravagantly decorated marble altar.

However, it's the outside of the Orsanmichele that is most famous. When it was built in its present form, the plan was to celebrate the commercial life of the city. Various guilds, representing trades ranging from bankers to wool merchants, commissioned the finest artists available to make statues of their respective patron saints, which were placed in 14 niches in the walls. Over the years, Ghiberti created a life-size bronze John the Baptist for the *Calimala* (cloth importers), Donatello sculpted St George for the Armourers (it's now in the Bargello) and Giambologna made St Luke for the Judges and Notaries. The statues you see today are copies: the originals are in the Orsanmichele Museum.

The piazza della Signoria is one of Florence's finest squares. Linked to piazza del Duomo by via dei Calzaiuoli – the city's main street in the Middle Ages – it has been the heart of civic life since the early 14th century and is rather like an open-air theatre that never closes.

The piazza was created in 1268, after the Guelphs defeated the Ghibellines, and buildings belonging to a prominent Ghibelline family were confiscated and left to fall into ruins as a visible reminder of their dastardly dealings. It grew larger when the Palazzo Vecchio was built to house the Signoria – the republican government. It's perhaps most famous as the site of the **Bonfire of the Vanities** on 7 February 1497, when the zealous monk Savonarola (1452-1498) – who had briefly become the city's ruler – ordered that sinful items (anything from mirrors and board games to priceless paintings and books) should be burned. He already operated a sort of religious police, who forced people to dress modestly and observe religious fasts, and even encouraged children to inform on their families. The bonfire was the high point of Savonarola's power. A few months later he was excommunicated, and in 1498 the Florentines turned against him: Savonarola was burned at the stake in this same piazza.

You'll see many statues in the square. There's a copy of Michelangelo's *David* in front of the Palazzo Vecchio, as well as the enormous **Neptune Fountain** (1575), in which a muscular Neptune (who from a certain angle looks, let's say, very pleased to see you) stands surrounded by water nymphs. Michelangelo declared that the sculptor, Bartolomeo Ammannati, had ruined a good piece of marble, and Florentines call Neptune *Il Biancone* – Big Whitey. There's also an equestrian statue of the Medici ruler Cosimo I, by Giambologna. Other statues fill the neighbouring **Loggia dei Lanzi**, including Giambologna's *Rape of the Sabine Women* (1583), sculpted from one enormous piece of marble, and Benvenuto Cellini's bronze *Perseus* (1554) who holds Medusa's head aloft.

The best people-watching spot is outside Rivoire. OK, the coffee's expensive but the seats afford an excellent view of the Palazzo Vecchio and the piazza.

Palazzo Vecchio
ⓘ *Piazza della Signoria, T055-276 8224/276 8325, www.comune.fi.it, Fri-Wed 0900-2400, Thu 0900-1400, €6.50, 18-25s €4.50, 3-17s free; tower €6.50; Studiolo di Francesco I tour €8.50.*
The building of this forbidding, fortress-like structure – which was designed by Arnolfo di Cambio – began in 1299 and was completed by the early 14th century. It was the centre of power in Florence and is still the city hall. The nine *Priori*, or republican rulers, lived here while in office, as did the Medici when Cosimo I moved here in 1540. It was originally called the Palazzo dei Priori, but when Cosimo later moved to the Pitti Palace on the other side of the Arno, this building became known as the Palazzo Vecchio, the Old Palace.

The interior still largely reflects Cosimo's era. He was keen to put his stamp on the palace and particularly wanted to eradicate anything that celebrated the republic, so employed Vasari, his court architect, to transform it. The lavishness is immediately evident while you queue to have your bags put through airport-style security in the courtyard, which was started by Michelozzo in the 15th century and later embellished by Vasari. In 2010, excavations revealed the remains of Florence's **Roman theatre** ⓘ *access by guided tour only, Sat-Sun €8, concessions €6.50, 8-18s €4 (under 8s not permitted); tour price includes access to the palace; book at ticket desk or T055-276 8224/8558*, beneath the Palazza Vecchio.

Walking tour of Florence

Start your tour at **Sant'Ambrogio market** on piazza Ghiberti. It's where locals come to buy their fruit and vegetables and is particularly lively early in the morning. Now walk down via de' Macci, turn right down via di San Giuseppe and you'll come to **Santa Croce**, where everyone from Michelangelo to Machiavelli is buried. You should be nice and early so you can beat the crowds if you intend to go inside (but allow – at least! – 90 minutes for a visit). If you're not going in, wander on to the piazza and admire the church's dazzling façade.

Now, if you want to visit some leather workshops, leave the piazza by Borgo de' Greci – it's lined with them. Or if you fancy an ice cream, turn left down via de' Benci and right into via dei Neri, where you'll find **Gelateria dei Neri**, which even offers soya ices. Either street will eventually bring you on to via Leoni – follow this round and you'll come into the **piazza della Signoria**, the civic heart of Florence where Savaronola held his Bonfire of the Vanities. Looking over the piazza is the forbidding Palazzo Vecchio, which dates back to the end of the 13th century – you'll need to allow a couple of hours for a visit, so settle instead for a coffee at Rivoire and a look at the statues in the square, notably the copy of Michelangelo's *David*.

The **Uffizi Gallery** is just off piazza della Signoria, but leave it for another day (you'll need to allow at least three hours) and walk along via Vacchereccia to the **Mercato Nuovo**, where you can browse for bags and belts and rub the nose of *Il Porcellino*, the bronze boar who sits here. Walk along via Porta Rossa to the **Palazzo Davanzati** (which you can visit if you get there before lunch): it's one of

Florence's lesser-known sights and gives an intriguing insight into medieval life. Continue to piazza Trinità and turn left to cross the **ponte Santa Trinità** – a great place to get photos of the **Ponte Vecchio**. For lunch you could now continue over the bridge to the **Oltrarno**, perhaps for a tasting plate at **Olio & Convivium** (via di Santo Spirito), or go back over the bridge and have a lunch at a café such as **Mangiafoco** on Borgo Santissimi Apostoli.

After lunch, time for some window-shopping along **via dei Tornabuoni**, which is crammed with designer names, then turn right at the top and walk along to the **piazza del Duomo**. The cathedral itself takes some time to explore, especially if you want to climb up inside **Brunelleschi's dome**. However, you should have time to visit the **Baptistery**, probably the oldest building in Florence. A short walk north now will take you to the **Palazzo Medici-Riccardi**, where the Medici lived before they moved into the Palazzo Vecchio. Pop in and see the frescoes in the **Chapel of the Magi**. Continue walking north, along via Cavour, and you'll come to **San Marco**, the monastic complex funded by Cosimo de' Medici. It was to here that Savonarola fled before he was arrested, and here that Fra Angelico painted delicate devotional frescoes on the walls of the monks' cells. It is one of the city's most atmospheric spots.

Before you head back into the city centre, take a walk along via Cesare Battisti to piazza Santissima Annunziata, Florence's elegant Renaissance square. The **Basilica della Santissima Annunziata** holds a special place in the hearts of local people – inside you'll find one of the most revered shrines in the city.

Salone dei Cinquecento Walk upstairs and you come to this vast room, the Hall of the Five Hundred, which was originally the meeting place for the representatives of Florence's republic. The gilded ceiling is covered in richly decorated panels celebrating the wonders of the Medici and the history of Florence – with Cosimo depicted like a Roman emperor. You can also see Michelangelo's statue *The Genius of Victory*.

The room practically echoes with the thunder of horses' hooves, as the walls are covered in Vasari's frescoes illustrating Florentine (and Medici) military triumphs over Pisa and Siena. Originally Michelangelo and Leonardo were commissioned to paint battle scenes here: the former the *Battle of Cascina*, the latter the *Battle of Anghiari*. However Michelangelo had completed only the cartoon or preparatory drawing for his fresco when Pope Julius II summoned him to Rome. As conventional frescoes had to be painted very quickly on wet plaster, Leonardo instead tried out an ancient technique known as *encausto* or encaustic painting, in which pigment was mixed with wax, to give himself more time to work. However, he had to use fires to keep the walls warm enough to work – and the wax melted and dripped. Leonardo abandoned the fresco and it was traditionally thought that Vasari simply painted over it, but some now think that he saved it by covering it with a thin wall. The search is on to find the lost Leonardo.

Studiolo di Francesco I If you are not on a special tour, you will only be able to peep into this jewel box of a room, in which every surface seems adorned with gilded and painted panels. However, on the Secret Passages tour you can see it properly and get a real insight into the strange world of the Medici. This windowless room was the private studio of Francesco, Cosimo I's son, who was fascinated by alchemy. Designed by Vasari, it was decorated by 30 artists, and each wall is dedicated to one of the four elements – Air, Fire, Water and Earth. The lowest paintings conceal secret cupboards in which Francesco kept his precious objects.

Another room on the Secret Passages tour is Cosimo's study, much smaller than his son's, with a secret door and places where he hid his jewellery, potions and glassware. Also on this floor are the rooms of Leo X, lavishly decorated with frescoes.

Quartiere di Eleonora di Toledo On the next level, if you turn left, you come to the **Quartiere degli Elementi**, a series of rooms decorated by Vasari. You can peep into the **Scrittoio della Calliope** (Calliope Study), dedicated to the Muses – if you look behind the door you can just see a rare stained glass window made by Walter of Antwerp, from a drawing by Vasari. Make sure you go on to the Terrazzo di Giunone and the Terrazzo di Saturno – the views are lovely.

If you turn right, you walk high above the Salone dei Cinquecento and enter the apartments of Eleonora di Toledo, the 18-year-old wife of Cosimo I. The tiny chapel is covered in paintings by Bronzino.

Sala dei Gigli You will next come to the **Sala dell'Udienza** (Audience Hall), with its imposing blue and golden ceiling, and then enter the **Sala dei Gigli** (Room of the Lilies), which gets its name from the fleurs-de-lys on the walls and boasts beautiful frescoes by Ghirlandaio. It's here that you'll find Donatello's bronze statue of *Judith and Holofernes* (c1460), which once stood in the piazza della Signoria.

Map room This was originally the *guarderoba*, where a variety of precious items were stored. It is covered with maps, by Egnazio Danti, depicting the known world in the mid-

Don't miss in the Uffizi

Giotto's *Madonna Enthroned*
The Duke and Duchess of Urbino
by Piero della Francesca
Botticelli's *Birth of Venus*
Michelangelo's *Holy Family*

The Annunciation by Leonardo da Vinci
Raphael's *Madonna of the Goldfinch*
Titian's *Venus of Urbino*
Filippo Lippi's *Madonna and Child with Two Angels*

16th century: one shows Nova Spagna, which is possibly California. The maps are on panels, arranged in blocks of four. Look at the top left corner of the bottom right panel in each set, and you will see a little slot for a key – the panels conceal cupboards. Behind 'Armenia' is a secret door: the palace is filled with hidden corridors that allowed the rulers to move around without anyone seeing them.

Before you reach the exit you can visit the oldest part of the palace. These rooms contain the Loeser Bequest paintings, but it's worth just taking a look at the rooms themselves with their brightly painted wooden ceilings. In the last one, behind a thick wooden door, is a stone toilet.

Galleria degli Uffizi

ⓘ *Piazzale degli Uffizi, T055-238 8651, www.firenzemusei.it; Tue-Sun 0815-1850, Jul-Sep may open until 2200 Tue-Wed, €6.50, EU citizens (with passport) 18-25s/over 65s €3.25, under 18s free; €11/€5.50 during special exhibitions; pre-book on T055-294883, at ticket office or on www.polomuseale.firenze.it or www.b-ticket.com (€4 booking fee); lift at entrance.*

Uffizi means 'offices', and this enormous, strength-sapping gallery was built by Vasari to provide administrative offices for Cosimo I. His heirs began to display their enormous collection of artworks here, and the last Medici heiress left it to the city. It contains the world's finest collection of Renaissance art and is crammed with masterpieces. Allow at least three hours for a visit and accept that you just won't see everything. Work is under way to expand the exhibition space, so don't be surprised if some rooms are closed or the layout is changed when you visit.

The main rooms are all upstairs, leading off two long corridors with ceilings painted in brilliant colours and walls lined with portraits and statues. Most of the collection is arranged chronologically, showing the development of Florentine art.

Rooms 2-10 The most important works in **Room 2** are the three altarpieces of the *Madonna Enthroned*, by Cimabue, Duccio and Giotto. They show how artists gradually broke away from the flat, idealized images that characterized Byzantine art and began to depict their subjects as real human beings. By the time you get to Giotto's work, which probably came from Ognissanti Church (see page 49), you can see real depth and softer, more natural poses.

Room 3 contains 14th-century Sienese works, notably a gilded *Annunciation* by Simone Martini, as well as paintings by the Lorenzetti brothers. In **rooms 5** and **6** you'll find works illustrating the international Gothic style, in particular Gentile da Fabriano's *Adoration of the Magi* (1423). This richly gilded painting was commissioned by a rival of the Medici for his private chapel, to show off his wealth.

Room 7 contains works of the early Renaissance, with paintings by Fra Angelico, Masaccio and a rare piece by Domenico Veneziano. His *Madonna and Child with Saints*, created for the Church of Santa Lucia, marks a move away from gilding in its use of pastel shades and soft, natural light. Veneziano died destitute in Florence. In **Room 8**, all attention is on Piero della Francesca's panels depicting the Duke and Duchess of Urbino. They look extremely human. There are several works by Fra Filippo Lippi, including a particularly beautiful *Madonna and Child with Two Angels* (c1465). The model is thought to have been Lucrezia Buti, a nun with whom Lippi, a monk but a notorious womanizer, was in love. He ran away with her and they set up home – their son was Filippino Lippi.

Room 9 contain works by Antonio and Piero Pollaiolo, who were willing to experiment with art. Antonio was noted for his anatomical observation.

Rooms 10-14 This is really one room, which showcases the paintings of Sandro Botticelli, most famously *The Birth of Venus* (c1484) in which Venus stands naked in a seashell being blown to land by the breath of Zephyrus. There is also *Primavera* (c1482), in which Venus stands in a wood surrounded by the three Graces, Flora, the goddess of Spring and Mercury.

Rooms 15-16 Here you can see early works by Leonardo da Vinci. There is the *Baptism of Christ in the Jordan* (c1473-1478) on which he collaborated with his teacher, Andrea del Verrocchio. It's thought that he painted his *Annunciation* (c1472) while he was still working in Verrocchio's studio. In it, Mary no longer sits in her bedroom as she did in earlier Annunciations; she is now in a palace and the Angel Gabriel's wings look strong and powerful. Leonardo's other work, painted on wood, is the *Adoration of the Magi* (c1481). He never completed the work because he left for Milan in 1482. Peep into **Room 16**, and have a look at the map-covered walls.

Rooms 18-24 **Room 18**, also known as the Tribuna, is an octagonal room that contained the Medicis' favourite works. The walls are covered with red velvet, the cupola encrusted with mother of pearl. Works within it include a richly decorated table, a sculpture known as the Medici Venus and paintings by Bronzino and Pontormo. The other rooms on this corridor contain works by artists from Luca Signorelli in **Room 19** to the German masters Albrecht Dürer and Lucas Cranach in **Room 20**. **Room 24** contains miniatures.

You've now reached the side of the gallery that overlooks the Arno. From the window at the far end, at the top of the next corridor, you get a great view of the Ponte Vecchio and can clearly see the roof of the **Corridorio Vasariano**. This is the covered passage, over 500 m long, designed by Vasari to link the Palazzo Vecchio to the Pitti Palace, via the Ponte Vecchio. It allowed the Medici to come and go without anyone seeing them. You can sometimes join a tour of the corridor, but you must book in advance.

At the end of this corridor there's a terrace with a café; it's expensive but the views of the Duomo and the Palazzo Vecchio are superb. If you're out here at noon you'll hear the city's bells ringing.

Rooms 25-28 **Room 25** contains Michelangelo's *Holy Family* or *Doni Tondo* (1506-1508), a work that inspired Mannerist artists. Not only has he departed from convention by not placing Christ on the Virgin's lap, his figures have clearly been influenced by his studies of classical statuary.

For works by Raphael go into **Room 26**, where you can see the *Madonna of the Goldfinch* (c1505-1506), an extremely gentle painting in which the infant Christ strokes the head of a goldfinch held by John the Baptist. There is also a more mature work from 1518 – the portrait *Pope Leo X with Two Cardinals*.

Ten of the best free things to do in Florence

1 Have a picnic in the rose garden near San Miniato al Monte.
2 Visit the Antica Farmacia, Santa Maria Novella.
3 Get a cheesy photo taken rubbing the nose of Il Porcellino.
4 Admire Ghirlandaio's Last Supper in Ognissanti.
5 Listen to Gregorian chant at San Miniato al Monte.
6 Stand underneath the cupola of the Duomo and marvel at how Brunelleschi did it.
7 Stroll across the Ponte Santa Trinità at sunset.
8 See Pontormo's Mannerist masterpiece at Santa Felicità.
9 Go window-shopping on via dei Tornabuoni.
10 Soak up the atmosphere at Sant'Ambrogio fruit and veg market.

In **Room 28**, Titian's *Venus of Urbino* (1538) reclines naked on a rumpled bed – it's the biggest selling postcard in the gallery. It was painted, apparently, as a lesson in sensuality for the young (very – she was 11) bride of the Duke of Urbino.

Rooms 31-45 Works in these rooms range from Tintoretto's *Leda and the Swan* (c1550-1560) to paintings by Rubens and Rembrandt. The latter's works are in **Room 44**, where there are also some lovely Dutch landscapes. In **Room 45**, if you've lasted that long, you'll find some of Canaletto's unmistakable views of Venice.

Ponte Vecchio
The Old Bridge dates back to around 1345, and replaced an even older bridge built by the Romans. In 1944, when the Nazis blew up all the bridges in Florence to stall the Allies' advance, this was the only one to be spared. It retains its medieval appearance, lined with shops and apartments, giving it a pleasantly higgledy-piggledy appearance. At one time it was the haunt of butchers and tanners, but the smell became so bad in the late 16th century that they were evicted to make way for goldsmiths. The jewellers are still there today. If you cross the Arno at the next bridge up, the Ponte Santa Trinità, you'll not only get great views of the Ponte Vecchio but also escape the crowds.

Museo Nazionale del Bargello
ⓘ *Via del Proconsolo 4, T055-238 8606, www.firenzemusei.it; Tue-Sun and 1st, 3rd and 5th Mon of each month 0815-1650, €6, EU citizens (with passport)/18-25s/over 65s €2, under 18s free; €7 during special exhibitions; pre-book on T055-294883 or www.polomuseale.firenze.it. (€4 booking fee).*
Just a short walk from piazza della Signoria, the Bargello is Florence's principal museum of sculpture. A forbidding building from the outside, it dates back to 1255, when it served as the seat of the Capitano del Popolo, the commander of the local militia. By 1271 it was the home of the Podestà (the chief magistrate), and it eventually became a court, prison and torture chamber. The Medici later made it the seat of the Bargello, the chief of police. It continued to serve as a prison until 1857, after which it was completely restored, becoming a museum of sculpture in 1859. The inner courtyard makes a striking contrast to the severe exterior, with arcades, coats of arms, a romantic upper loggia and – in summer – swallows swooping overhead. It's hard to believe that it was once the site of the city's gallows.

The area opposite the entrance is used for temporary exhibitions. Upstairs on the first floor are carved ivories dating from the fifth to the 17th centuries – perhaps the most famous item is the ninth-century *flabellum*, or fan, which kept insects away from the altar during religious ceremonies. Other rooms contain majolica ware, Islamic art and 13th- and 14th-century sculptures by Arnolfo di Cambio and Tino da Camaino.

Displayed in the loggia are the Flemish sculptor Giambologna's bronze birds, made for the Medici. The main room on this level is notable for its works by Donatello. The most important sculptor of the 15th century, Donatello – who trained as a goldsmith and then worked for a while in Ghiberti's studio – combined great technical ability with enormous expressiveness. Here you can see his original *St George* (1416-1417), carved for a niche on the Orsanmichele (see page 33), and the restored *Amore-Attis* (c1440) – a quirky figure wearing a thick belt, sandals and a rather wicked expression. Pride of place goes to his slim, beautiful and rather camp bronze *David* (1440s). Carved for the Medici, this was the first freestanding nude statue in Western art since classical times. Other works include the panels made by Brunelleschi and Ghiberti as entries for the competition to make the doors of the Baptistery (see page 29).

Downstairs, beside the entrance, is a room displaying works by Michelangelo, Cellini and Giambologna. Compare Michelangelo's tipsy marble *Bacchus* (1496-1497), with grapes cascading from his head, with Giambologna's version.

San Marco → *For listings, see pages 53-64.*

There's an almost constant stream of tourists to the area around piazza San Marco – all desperate to tick Michelangelo's *David* off their 'must see' list. However, a surprising number don't stay around to visit the area's other glorious sight – the Museo di San Marco, a Dominican monastery lovingly frescoed by Fra Angelico.

Galleria dell'Accademia
ⓘ *Via Ricasoli 60, T055-238 8612, www.firenzemusei.it; Tue-Sun 0815-1850, Jul-Sep may open until 2200 Tue-Thu, €6.50, EU citizens (with passport)/18-25s €3.25, under 18s/over 65s free; €11/€5 during special exhibitions; pre-book on T055-294883 or www.polomuseale.firenze. it (€4 booking fee).*
The Accademia started life as the Accademia di Belle Arti, an art school that gradually developed its own collection of artworks. Today around a million visitors a year are said to beat a path here – all to see just one statue.

It's strange to think that the Carrara marble from which Michelangelo's *David*, probably the world's most famous statue, was carved had been rejected by other artists as unworkable – too thin, cracked and discoloured. It lay in storage, rather battered, until Michelangelo asked if he could try his hand. He was only in his mid-20s. The Opera del Duomo commissioned him and he started work in 1501. By 1504 this huge statue (over 4 m high) was completed.

It attracted controversy from the outset. This powerful-looking David, capable of defeating Goliath, symbolized the new republican Florence – recently freed from the rule of both the Medici family and Savonarola. When the statue was moved into place on the piazza della Signoria, it was attacked by mobs of Medici sympathizers. David got rather battered over the years. His left arm was smashed during a riot in 1527, and he was pounded by the elements. He was moved to the Accademia for protection in 1873, but was attacked in 1991 by an Italian painter, who smashed his toe with a hammer.

Stand beneath the mighty statue today and you're sure to be struck by David's outsize hands and rather large head. This was deliberate, as Michelangelo intended him to stand high up on the Duomo and to be viewed from far below. You might also notice that he isn't particularly well endowed. There is a theory that this too is deliberate: this David (unlike Donatello's earlier version) is not a young boy who has just killed a giant, he's an athletic man preparing for a fight, and every anatomical detail is considered to be correct – including a 'manhood' that has shrivelled with fear. A screen next to the statue allows you to view parts of it in detail, such as the unusual heart-shaped pupils of his eyes.

Recently there has been concern that the statue is in danger of cracking, due to the vibrations of the millions of feet that pass it each day. Some have suggested that it should be removed to a new site, outside the city centre; others want to insulate it at a cost of around €1m.

The rest of the collection The Accademia is also home to a plaster model of Giambologna's *Rape of the Sabines* and two fascinating incomplete works by Michelangelo. Known as the *Slaves*, or *Prisoners*, they were intended for the tomb of Pope Julius II but were never completed. They clearly show how a sculpture would emerge from a piece of stone, like a prisoner escaping.

In another room, devoted to 14th-century art, there's a gilded *Tree of Life* (1310-1315) by Pacino di Buonaguida, in which Christ's ancestry is lovingly portrayed. The Accademia also contains a **Museum of Musical Instruments** (turn right as you go in). If you're lucky you might happen upon an ensemble playing the instruments in rehearsal for a concert.

Museo di San Marco

① *Piazza San Marco 3, T055-238 8608, www.firenzemusei.it; Mon-Fri 0815-1350, Sat 0815-1850, Sun 0815-1900 (open 1st, 3rd and 5th Mon of each month and 2nd and 4th Sun), €4, EU citizens (with passport)/18-25s €2, under 18s/over 65s free; pre-book on T055-294883 or www.polomuseale.firenze.it (€3 booking fee).*

Founded in 1436, this Dominican monastery was built with generous funds from the devout Medici, Cosimo il Vecchio ('the Elder'). He engaged the architect Michelozzo to create an elegant complex for the order, which had moved here from Fiesole. The whole place exudes a gentle piety, with tranquil cloisters and walls that seem to whisper their history as you pass. The most important works are undoubtedly the frescoes painted by one of the monastery's inmates – the monk and talented artist Fra Angelico. His works were intended to inspire devotion and contemplation, and have a remarkable ethereal quality.

You come first to Michelozzo's cool, green Sant'Antonio cloister, on one wall of which you can see Fra Angelico's *St Dominic at the Cross* (c1442). The former Pilgrim's Hospice, to the right of the entrance, is filled with panel paintings by Fra Angelico, taken from churches and monasteries all over Florence. They include the *Pala di San Marco* (c1438-1443) considered the prototype Renaissance altarpiece, which was commissioned by Cosimo il Vecchio for the monastery church.

Awaiting you at the top of the stairs is Fra Angelico's masterpiece – his immensely moving *Annunciation* (c1442). The Virgin and the Angel Gabriel gently bend towards one another beneath the arches of a loggia resembling that created by Michelozzo. There are more lovingly painted frescoes in the monks' cells that line the corridors. Those on the left wall are by Fra Angelico himself; the others follow his design. The first cell on the left has a *Noli mi Tangere*, in which Christ appears to Mary Magdalene in a garden – the landscape featuring prominently in the picture. The fifth cell on the left-hand side has a *Nativity* scene and cell 6 has a luminous *Transfiguration*. If you walk along the next corridor you come to the cells occupied by Savonarola, the Dominican friar who ordered the Bonfire of the Vanities (see page 34). There are fragments of his clothes, including a black cloak, his rosary and a painting of him being burned at the stake in the piazza della Signoria. If you turn right and go to the end, you'll come to a comparatively plush set of cells reserved for Cosimo Il Vecchio. Back downstairs, the Small Refectory has a fresco of the *Last Supper* (c1479-1480) on the end wall. It's by Ghirlandaio and is considered to be the twin of the one he painted in the Ognissanti (see page 49).

Piazza Santissima Annunziata

This lovely square, close to San Marco, is famed for the elegantly restrained nine-arched loggia of the **Spedale degli Innocenti**. This was Europe's first foundling hospital, designed by Brunelleschi around 1419. Above the arches you can see Andrea della Robbia's blue terracotta roundels depicting babies – designed to encourage charitable giving – which were added in the 1480s. Later there was a small revolving door in the wall, where babies could be left anonymously.

The **Santissima Annunziata** ① *T055-266181, daily 0730-1230 and 1600-1750, free*, is surely the most extraordinary church in Florence, gilded and elaborately decorated like a dark-coloured opera house. The walls of the cloisters, which you walk through on your way in, are covered with frescoes – the earliest is a *Nativity* painted in 1460 by Alesso Baldovinetti, and there are others by Andrea del Sarto. When you go into the church it seems almost back to front, as there's an ornate shrine to the left of the entrance that looks at first like the altar. It was built to house a 14th-century painting of the Virgin that was said to have been completed by angels and was credited with many miracles.

Giardino dei Semplici

① *Via Micheli 3, www.msn.unifi.it, summer Thu-Tue 1000-1900, winter Sat-Mon 1000-1700, €6.* If you want to escape the crowds for a while, visit this botanical garden near San Marco, established by Cosimo I to research medicinal plants. Now part of the University of Florence's **Natural History Museum**, it makes a pleasant place to stroll and snooze. The entry price also gets you in to the other sections of the museum.

Around San Lorenzo → For listings, see pages 53-64.

Squeezed between Santa Maria Novella and San Marco, this part of Florence is closely associated with the Medici; this was where they lived, where they worshipped and where they are buried. It's an immensely lively area, due not only to its proximity to the main station, but also to the presence of a busy street market and the Mercato Centrale, the covered food market.

Basilica di San Lorenzo

ⓘ *Piazza San Lorenzo, T055-264 5184, Mon-Sat 1000-1730, Sun 1330-1730, closed Sun Nov-Mar, €4.50.*

The Church of San Lorenzo is the oldest church in Florence. Founded in AD 393, it once served as Florence's cathedral – before Santa Reparata, the church now buried beneath the Duomo, took over. In later years it became the parish church of the wealthy Medici family. In 1419 Giovanni di Bicci de' Medici offered to pay for a new church and commissioned Brunelleschi to carry out the work. Brunelleschi died before he could complete it, and the building was finished by another architect, possibly Antonio Manetti. In the 16th century, the Medici Pope Leo X commissioned Michelangelo to create a grand marble façade and a plan was drawn up, but the project was later abandoned and the church remains unfinished to this day.

The most important works inside are the bronze pulpits, the last works of Donatello, which are carved in a free, unfinished style, like dramatic sketches. He died before he completed them and they were finished by his pupils. Donatello is buried in the church, beside his patron Cosimo il Vecchio. Then there's the **Sagrestia Vecchia** (the Old Sacristy), which was one of Brunelleschi's first works. It was decorated by Donatello and contains Medici tombs.

Cappelle Medicee

ⓘ *Piazza Madonna degli Aldobrandini, T055-238 8602, www.firenzemusei.it; Tue-Sat and 1st, 3rd and 5th Sun of each month, 0815-1350 (may close earlier out of season), €6 (€9 until 6 Oct 2013), EU citizens (with passport) 18-25s, €3 (€4.50 until 6 Oct 2013), under 18s/over 65s free; pre-book on T055-294883 or www.b-ticket.com (€3 booking fee).*

Part of San Lorenzo, but reached by a separate entrance, the Medici Chapel is the mausoleum where many members of the family are buried. You go upstairs to the **Capella dei Principi**, the Chapel of the Princes. The most expensive project the family ever funded, it gives the impression that they were trying to take their money with them when they died. It certainly shows that money can't buy you taste – it is a jaw-dropping mix of marble and grey stone, inlaid with coral, mother-of-pearl and lapis lazuli. Work began in 1604 and the Medici, never ones to think small, intended that the Holy Sepulchre itself would be brought here from Jerusalem and laid alongside them. The authorities in the Holy Land refused. The family continued to lavish money on their mausoleum until the last of the line died in 1743. The Chapel of the Princes wasn't completed until 1962, when the floor was finished. Unfortunately, much of it is covered in scaffolding as the chapel is undergoing renovations.

From here you come into the **Sagrestia Nuova**, the New Sacristy. This predates the Chapel of the Princes – work began in 1520 – and is decidedly more restrained. Michelangelo designed it as well as the Medici tombs inside. The most eye-catching tombs, which he worked on alone, are of those of two minor Medici: that of Lorenzo, Duke of Urbino, is topped with allegorical figures of Dusk and Dawn; while that of Giuliano, Duke of Nemours, is topped with Night and Day.

Also here is the large, unfinished tomb of Lorenzo the Magnificent and his brother Giuliano. Michelangelo intended that this should be decorated with river gods and other figures. However, he only got as far as carving the Madonna and Child before going to Rome.

Palazzo Medici-Riccardi
ⓘ *Via Cavour 3, T055-276 0340, www.palazzo-medici.it, Mon-Tue and Thu-Sun 0900-1900, €7/€4, under 6s free, admission to Cappella dei Magi restricted to 8 visitors every 7 mins: book in advance by phone.*

You might think this building looks unimpressive from the outside, dull even. That was deliberate: Cosimo il Vecchio was too astute to flaunt his wealth to all and sundry. He had originally asked Brunelleschi to design this, the family's first serious palace in Florence, but the architect came up with a grandiose plan that Cosimo rejected as "too sumptuous and magnificent and liable to stir envy among the populace". Cosimo turned instead to Michelozzo, who designed this restrained Renaissance residence that managed to look intimidating and yet elegant. And inside they were free to enjoy more lavish decor.

The Medici had moved to Florence from the Mugello (see page 65), and in the mid-14th century, when they were making money from banking, bought a number of properties in this area of the city. It was around 1445 that Cosimo commissioned this palace. In the 17th century it was sold to the Riccardi family, who enlarged and altered it. The courtyard, designed by Michelozzo, has columns in *pietra serena* (a grey stone) and arches festooned with carvings. You can walk from here into the quiet garden, with statues and citrus fruits.

Cappella dei Magi
The Chapel of the Magi is upstairs, and is the palace's main attraction. It was completed by Michelozzo in 1459, after which a pupil of Fra Angelico's, Benozzo Gozzoli, began to decorate the walls. He covered them with jewel-coloured frescoes, ostensibly telling the story of the *Procession of the Magi* but in reality immortalizing members of the Medici family as they took part in the annual procession of the wealthy Florentine confraternity, the Compagnia dei Magi. It's a fascinating idealized pageant set in a rocky landscape – the gentry, straight-backed on horseback, are accompanied by pages, cheetahs, wild birds and camels.

You can pick out various individuals. Most think that the young man on the east wall, wearing gold and riding a white horse, is a young Lorenzo the Magnificent. Behind him is Cosimo il Vecchio, wearing a black cloak, and just in front of him, on another white horse, Piero de' Medici, who commissioned the work. Look carefully at the crowd of followers and you can see the artist himself (his name is written on his red hat).

Other rooms upstairs in the palace are the **Sala delle Quattro Stagioni**, which gets its name from the 17th-century tapestries designed by Lorenzo Lippi, and the 18th-century **Sala Luca Giordano**, its ceiling a blue and white puff of clouds on which sit the last of the Medici. In another room is the rather more tasteful *Madonna and Child* by Filippo Lippi, painted when he was probably too old to chase women any more.

Mercato Centrale
The streets around San Lorenzo church are filled with stalls selling items such as belts and bags, sunglasses and souvenirs. The Mercato Centrale nearby is the main food market. It's a covered market built in the 19th century, and worth visiting whether you're putting together a picnic or just looking to soak up some city atmosphere. Stalls sell meat, vegetables, cheese and pasta, and there are plenty of cheap eating places nearby. Look out for the tripe sellers – it's fast food Florentine-style.

Santa Croce and around → *For listings, see pages 53-64.*

Piazza Santa Croce is one of Florence's liveliest squares – a great place to picnic and people-watch. Each year it becomes a stadium for the Calcio Storico, a no-holds-barred football match played in medieval costume. This area was particularly badly hit when the Arno flooded Florence in 1966 – you can see a mark showing the height the water reached near the corner with via de'Benci.

Basilica di Santa Croce

ⓘ *Piazza Santa Croce, T055-246 6105, Mon-Sat 0930-1730, Sun 1430-1730, €6 (includes museum).*

The largest Franciscan church in the world, this vast building – the burial place of Ghiberti, Galileo, Machiavelli and Michelangelo – can easily occupy two or three hours of your time. Its size reflects the fact that the Franciscans were a popular preaching order and needed a large space to accommodate their congregation. You can see the Dominican equivalent on the opposite side of the city, at Santa Maria Novella (see page 48).

Santa Croce is often known as the Pantheon of Florence. There's so much to see that it's easy to understand why the writer Stendhal was quite overcome when he visited in 1817: "Upon leaving Santa Croce my heart was beating irregularly...life was ebbing out of me and I went forwards in fear of swooning." The term Stendhal's Syndrome is now used to describe the sort of masterpiece overload that you can experience in Florence.

The most accepted date for the church's construction is 1294, though the façade wasn't completed until the 19th century. The architect was Arnolfo di Cambio, but the building was later re-modelled by Vasari, who painted over many early frescoes. The church is currently being restored and you might find that some items of interest are covered up, but there'll still be plenty to see. You enter by the side entrance, not through the main doors in the piazza.

Family chapels While it was not 'done' for wealthy families to flaunt their money in Renaissance Florence, it was acceptable for them to pay for works within a church or cathedral. This made them appear pious and benevolent – but it also gave them an opportunity to show just how rich they were, commissioning the greatest artists and sculptors of the day to decorate private chapels and tombs. To the right of the altar you can see the **Bardi Chapel** and the **Peruzzi Chapel**, both covered with frescoes by Giotto. Compare the 13th-century gilded altarpiece in the Bardi Chapel with Giotto's frescoes on the wall and you can trace the burgeoning artistic revolution. In the altar panel Saint Francis is portrayed in rigid Byzantine manner and the scenes around him are stylized, with the most important figures painted taller than the others, while in the fresco depicting the death of St Francis the characters are realistically proportioned, and their grief is obvious from their faces and postures.

To the left of the altar you should usually be able to see a wooden crucifix by Donatello (1420). The arms are inventively hinged, enabling it to serve as either a crucifixion or a deposition.

Cappella Baroncelli This chapel, at the end of the transept, has frescoes (c1332) by Taddeo Gaddi, assistant to Giotto. They include a rare night scene depicting the *Annunciation to the Shepherds*, and scenes from the *Life of the Virgin* on the main chapel wall. In the panel on the bottom right is a priest deciding who should marry Mary.

Joseph brandishes a leafy branch with a dove above it, pleased that he's won her hand, while a man at the front of the picture snaps a branch beneath his foot, annoyed that he wasn't chosen. In the altar, the central panel showing the coronation of the Virgin is attributed to Giotto.

Cappella Rinuccini A corridor leads to the Sacristy, which contains a *Crucifixion* by Taddeo Gaddi and a huge wooden table on which the body of Michelangelo lay in state – he died in Rome, but was brought back to Florence to be buried. Behind railings is the **Rinuccini Chapel**, which contains scenes from the *Life of the Virgin* by a follower of Giotto. The wall by the entrance is painted in imitation of marble. If you look at the bottom, in the middle, you can see that one of the artists has painted himself.

Famous tombs At the back of the church (furthest from the altar), above the tomb of Niccolini, is a statue that is believed to have been the inspiration for the Statue of Liberty. Nearby, on the south aisle, is Michelangelo's tomb, which was designed by Vasari and is topped with allegorical figures representing painting, sculpture and architecture. Michelangelo died in 1564, which was the year Galileo was born, so Galileo's tomb was placed on the opposite aisle. There is a bust of the 'heretical' scientist holding a telescope. Next to Michelangelo's tomb is Dante's, although the great writer isn't buried here but in Ravenna where he had been exiled. Carved in the 19th century, the tomb is often mocked by Florentines, who joke that Dante looks as if he is sitting on the toilet.

Beside Dante is the tomb of the poet Vittorio Alfieri, carved by Canova. Known for living the good life and occasionally tying himself to his desk to force himself to work, Alfieri ran away with Bonnie Prince Charlie's wife, the Countess of Albany. She is said to have modelled for the figure representing Italy on top of the tomb. The towers of San Gimignano form a crown on her head.

The cloister Leaving the main church through the cloister, you come to the **Cappella de' Pazzi**, which was designed by Brunelleschi for the wealthy Pazzi family of bankers and begun in the early 1440s. It's an example of harmonious design, with simple geometric forms and decorations by Desiderio da Settignano and Luca della Robbia.

Finally you come to the museum, in the former monastic refectory. Among its highlights are Cimabue's famous *Crucifix*, which was badly damaged in the floods of 1966, as well as a glorious fresco of the *Tree of the Cross and Last Supper* (c1333) by Taddeo Gaddi.

Museo Horne

ⓘ *Via dei Benci 6, just south of piazza Santa Croce, by the Arno, T055-244661, www. museohorne.it, Mon-Sat 0900-1300, €6.*

Housed in the Palazzo Corsi, a visit to this museum gives you a chance to see a typical wealthy cloth merchant's dwelling of the Renaissance. The house doubled as business premises, and cloth that had been dyed down in the cellars would have been hung up to dry high above the courtyard. The building was saved in the 19th century by an English art historian, Percy Horne, who restored it and filled it with a collection of artworks and quirky objects. He left it to the state when he died in 1916. Look out for features like the original glass in the windows and thick wooden shutters.

On the first floor there's *St Catherine of Alexandria* by Luca Signorelli and a painting of *Three Saints* that is an early work by Pietro Lorenzetti. Dominating one wall is an unfinished *Deposition* by Benozzo Gozzoli, one of the earliest examples of oil on canvas. Near a portrait of Percy Horne there's a *Crucifixion* by Filippino Lippi. Other rooms contain Giotto's *St Stephen* and a *cassone* or wedding chest: this wasn't just a box to store valuables but also a place to sit or lie down.

On the next floor, in a former bedroom, there's a *lettuccio* – a 15th-century day bed. It looks like a huge seat but would have been covered with a mattress and covers, which were stored in a drawer beneath.

Around piazza della Repubblica → *For listings, see pages 53-64.*

This vast piazza, lined with famous cafés, was the site of the Roman forum and later the main marketplace. All was swept away when Florence briefly became capital in the 19th century, and the enormous triumphal arch was the first stage in the city's planned rebuilding. Nearby is the Mercato Nuovo, where tourists queue to rub the (very shiny) nose of the bronze boar, Il Porcellino – said to ensure a return to Florence.

Palazzo Davanzati

ⓘ *Via Porta Rossa 13, T055-238 8610, Tue-Sat, 1st, 3rd and 5th Sun and 2nd and 4th Mon of each month 0815-1350, pre-book on T055-238 8610 (€2).*

A short distance from the Mercato Nuovo, the Palazzo Davanzati was built in the mid-14th century by joining together existing properties. It's a fascinating example of a medieval merchant's home and remained in the hands of the Davanzati family until the 19th century.

You step into an outer loggia, which once served as a shop. If you look up you can see spy holes, covered with wood, so that the family could see what was happening down below. The inner courtyard has a romantic Romeo-and-Juliet quality, with a stunning staircase. You'll see that while the lower section of the staircase is made of stone, the higher sections are made of wood – no point using expensive materials when only the family would see them. There's a well here too – a system of ropes and pulleys meant water could be carried to all levels of the house.

Upstairs on the first floor, the Sala Madornale preserves a brightly painted ceiling, while the Sala dei Pappagalli gets its name because its walls are covered with parrots. Further round on this floor is the Camera de Pavani, a bedroom that once had peacocks on the walls and the medieval equivalent of an en suite bathroom.

The second floor can be seen only on pre-booked, guided tours. Up here there is another wooden ceiling and signs of ancient graffiti. The bedroom is covered in paintings of the mid-14th century depicting a tragic French love story, and you can also see items of furniture like *cassoni* (marriage chests) and a *desco da parto*, or 'birthing tray'. Roundels of this kind were made to carry refreshments to a mother after she had given birth. They were often elaborately painted and hung on bedroom walls as decoration.

Via de'Tornabuoni

Just west of Palazzo Davanzati, along via Porta Rossa, is the smartest shopping street in Florence, via de' Tornabuoni. *Pucci*, *Prada*, *Dior*, *Cartier*, *Armani* – you name them, they're here. The huge **Ferragamo** headquarters occupies its own palace by the Arno, near ponte Santa Trinità. If you've got a bit of a thing about shoes, go into their **museum** ⓘ *Wed-Mon 1000-1800, €5, under 10s/over 65s free*, where you can see items like the original lasts and the shoes they made for film stars such as Katharine Hepburn, Marilyn Monroe and Audrey Hepburn. Make sure you pop into the nearby **Church of Santa Trinita** ⓘ *free*, in piazza Santa Trinità. It's famed for Domenico Ghirlandaio's frescoes depicting the *Life of St Francis* (c1483-1486) in the Sassetti Chapel. Further along via dei Tornabuoni is **Palazzo Strozzi** ① *www.palazzostrozzi.org*, the largest palace in Florence, which was built for the Strozzi banking family. Temporary art exhibitions are held here, and you can wander into the courtyard, where there's a café.

Around piazza Santa Maria Novella → *For listings, see pages 53-64.*

This area of the city is dominated by the transport hub of Santa Maria Novella station and it is easy to overlook its attractions as you hurry to better-known sights such as the Duomo and the Uffizi. Yet one of the city's most important churches is here, sitting with its back to the station. Its façade has recently been restored and the piazza in front has been cleaned up, enabling it to present a bright new face to the world.

Santa Maria Novella
① *Piazza Santa Maria Novella, T055-264 5184, Mon-Thu and Sat 0900-1700, Fri 1100-1730, Sun 1300-1700, church, museum and Green Cloister €5.*
A church stood here as early as AD 983. In 1221 it was handed to the Dominicans. Around 1240 the friars themselves started building the church you see today, and it was consecrated in 1420. By then, however, only the lower part of the façade had been completed, in Romanesque style. In the 1450s Giovanni Rucellai paid for Leon Battista Alberti to finish the work, which he did in Renaissance style.

You enter the church by a side door, reached through the graveyard. Inside you'll initially be struck by the rather severe interior – a reminder that the Dominicans were the *domini canes*, or 'hounds of God' and tended to take a rigid approach to their faith – as evidenced by Savonarola. In addition, Vasari put his stamp on the church by painting over many of the original frescoes. However, this building is filled with treasures. On the opposite wall to the entrance is Masaccio's *Trinity* (1427) which demonstrates extraordinary skill with perspective, creating a stunning *trompe d'oeil*.

Hanging in the centre of the nave is a large wooden crucifix (c1290) by Giotto, back in its original position after restoration.

Around the altar To the right, steps lead up to the frescoed **Cappella Rucellai**, which contains a statue of the *Madonna and Child* (c1350) by Nino Pisano. Closer to the altar, on the right, are chapels that 'belonged' to wealthy families. First is the **Bardi Chapel**, with lunettes frescoed by Duccio di Buoninsegna (c1285) and, beside the altar, the beautiful **Filippo Strozzi Chapel**, which contains some of Filippino Lippi's finest frescoes (c1489-1502). The chancel, behind the altar, is decorated with a fresco cycle by Domenico Ghirlandaio (c1485-1490) commissioned by the banker Giovanni Tornabuoni. It depicts the lives of the Virgin and St John the Baptist. It functions as a sort of promotional panel for the Tornabuoni family, with Giovanni's daughter dressed in gold in the scene depicting the birth of the Virgin, and Lucrezia Tornabuoni, the mother of Lorenzo the Magnificent, attending the birth of St John the Baptist on the other wall. Moving to the left of the altar you can see a crucifix by Brunelleschi. Further round is the **Cappella Strozzi di Mantova**, reached by steps, depicting scenes from Dante's *Inferno*: Paradise on the left wall and Purgatory on the right.

Museum and Green Cloister The entrance to the museum is to the left of the façade. You come into the **Chiostro Verde** (Green Cloister), which was built between 1332 and 1362. The walls are covered with early 15th-century frescoes by Paolo Uccello and his assistants, and the cloister gets its name from the green pigment they used. The best-preserved image is of *Noah and the Flood*. Walk around the cloister and you reach the **Spanish Chapel**, which got its name because the court of the Spanish wife of Cosimo I worshipped here – it had previously been the headquarters of the Inquisition. Frescoes by Andrea Bonaiuti (c1365-1367) smother the walls. The right-hand wall depicts the *Allegory of the Triumph of the Church and the Dominican Order*, in which people indulge in dancing, picking forbidden fruit and being 'lusty', while disapproving Dominicans with their 'dogs of God' stand ready to force these sinners to repent. On the left of this image is a pink building, which may be how the artist imagined the Duomo would look when finished.

Chiesa di Ognissanti

ⓘ *Piazza Ognissanti, daily, refectory Mon, Tue, Sat 0900-1200, free.*

Ognissanti, or All Saints, church is just a short walk from Santa Maria Novella on a piazza down by the Arno. Founded in 1251 by the Umiliati, an order associated with the woollen industry, it was the parish church of the well-heeled Vespucci family. One of their members, the explorer Amerigo Vespucci, gave his name to America. He's said to be buried in the church, and his image is immortalized in Ghirlandaio's fresco of the *Madonna della Misericordia* (1470s) – he is the figure whose face is immediately to the left of the Madonna. Also buried in Ognissanti is the artist Sandro Botticelli, who painted the picture of *St Augustine* here.

However the most interesting work is in the **Refectory**, reached through quiet cloisters just to the left of the church. Here, on the far wall, is a *Last Supper* by Ghirlandaio, painted in 1480. Similar in composition, though less formal, than the one he painted in San Marco (see page 42), it's an intriguing scene filled with symbolic images. In the background there's a palm tree for martyrdom, orange trees for heaven and cypress trees for death. On the table itself are apricots for evil and cherries for Christ's blood, while a peacock perched above symbolizes immortality. Ghirlandaio (1449-1494) has been likened to a photographer because of the attention he gave to tiny details and his ability to create realistic images. He appears in this fresco himself – as the disciple at the far left end of the table.

The Oltrarno → *For listings, see pages 53-64.*

The district on the Arno's southern bank is a great place to find buzzing bars and restaurants off the tourist trail. Traditionally a working area, it's still famous for its artisans' workshops, where you can buy anything from handmade shoes to statues. The main visitor attraction is the Pitti Palace, but it's not the only sight of note – try to make time to see the frescoes in the Brancacci Chapel and, high on a hill to the east, the church of San Miniato al Monte – which one Florentine after another declares is their favourite spot in the whole city.

Palazzo Pitti

ⓘ *Piazza Pitti, www.polomuseale.firenze.it, the museums' opening hours vary; inclusive ticket €11.50/€5.75 (€9/€4.50 after 1600), valid for 3 days, not available during special exhibitions; pre-book on T055-294883 (€3 booking fee); concessions for EU citizens 18-25, EU citizens under 18/over 65 (on presentation of passport) free; bus 12 or 23 from Santa Maria Novella.*

The wealthy banker Luca Pitti built his palace as large as possible in an attempt to outshine the Medici, but when the Pitti fortunes declined, Cosimo I seized the opportunity to buy it for himself and made it his main residence. When Florence briefly became capital of a united Italy it became the royal residence.

The palace is divided into separate museums with separate prices and entry times. The main one is the Palatine Gallery, which takes you into the State Apartments. Extending behind the palace are the Boboli Gardens, perfect for a picnic.

Galleria Palatina
ⓘ *T055-238 8614, www.firenzemusei.it; Tue-Sun 0815-1850, €8.50/€4.25, EU citizens under 18/over 65 (on presentation of passport) free; includes the Galleria d'Arte Moderna (price may rise to €13/€6.50 during special exhibitions).*
The Palatine Gallery is on the first floor of the Pitti Palace and contains the Medici's extensive collection of artworks – particularly their paintings. You'll find works here by everyone from Fra Bartolomeo to Van Dyck. They're displayed as they would have been when they were acquired, so don't expect any chronological order. The rooms in which they hang are as fascinating as the paintings, as you pass through bedrooms, private sitting rooms and the bathroom of Napoleon's sister, who once lived here: there are grandiose chandeliers, baroque ceiling frescoes and ornate plasterwork.

Among the masterpieces on display are Filippo Lippi's *Madonna with Child* and *Episodes from the Life of St Anne* (c1450) and the *Child St John* (1523) by Andrea del Sarto. There are works by Salvator Rosa, Rubens and Caravaggio, as well as Velazquez. Perhaps the best-known works are in the rooms named after Venus, Apollo, Mars, Jupiter and Saturn. Here you'll find paintings by Raphael and Titian, including Raphael's *Madonna della Seggiola* ('Madonna of the chair') and his *La Velata* ('Veiled Woman') whom Vasari said was the artist's lover. The room of Venus contains Canova's sculpture of *Venus Italica*, commissioned by Napoleon in 1810.

The gallery leads into the Royal Apartments, which show a mix of decorative styles. After the Medici left, the rooms were renovated by the Dukes of Lorraine and then by Vittorio Emanuele II. They're a lavish succession of huge chandeliers, rich brocades, tapestries and fine furniture.

Galleria d'Arte Moderna
ⓘ *Opening hours and prices as Palatine Gallery.*
'Modern art' is 'late 18th- to early 20th-century art', as demonstrated by the works on the second floor of the Pitti Palace. The most important works are those by the Macchiaioli, the Italian division of the Impressionists: look out for landscapes and battle scenes in rooms 16 to 18. Of note is Giovanni Fattori's *Riposa* (1887), in which a farmer from the Maremma sits by the sea with his ox cart. Other rooms have paintings of the Risorgimento.

Museo degli Argenti
ⓘ *T055-238 8709; daily except 1st and last Mon of each month, Nov-Feb 0815-1630, Mar 0815-1730, Apr-May, Sep-Oct 0815-1830, Jun-Aug 0815-1930, €7/€3, EU citizens under 18/over 65 (on presentation of passport) free, includes Galleria del Costume, Museo delle Porcellane, Giardino Bardini and Giardino Boboli, may rise to €10/€5 during special exhibitions.*
On the ground floor of the palace, to the left of the main entrance, this is a succession of extraordinarily grand rooms that were part of the Medici summer apartments. Frescoes in the **Sala di Giovanni di San Giovanni** depict Lorenzo de' Medici giving refuge to the Muses, who have been chased from Paradise. Despite its name, the museum is not devoted to silverware but contains a range of precious (though not always pretty) objects such as ivories, glassware and amber.

Other museums covered by the same ticket are the **Museum of Costume**, with fashions from the 16th century to the present day, and the **Porcelain Museum**, on the far side of the Boboli Gardens.

Boboli Gardens
ⓘ *0815-dusk, prices as for Museo degli Argenti, last entry 1 hr before closing.*
The Medici started laying out the Boboli Gardens around 1550, and various architects contributed to their appearance. Over the years they were extended and remodelled, with successive palace residents putting their stamp on the gardens. In the 18th century they were opened to the public.

The gardens are a formal mix of tree-lined avenues, fountains and clipped lawns dotted with classical statues and follies. Down by the palace exit you can see a statue of Cosimo's court dwarf as Bacchus, sitting on a tortoise, and the Grotta di Buontalenti – a bubbling cluster of dripping stones within which is secreted Giambologna's *Venus*. Other features include the Amphitheatre, designed so the Medici could enjoy alfresco entertainment in Roman style, and the Isolotto, an island fountain in the centre of a lake.

Less well known and less crowded than the Boboli are the **Bardini Gardens**, reached through via de' Bardi. Features include an English woodland and a baroque stairway.

Chiesa di Santa Maria del Carmine – Cappella Brancacci
ⓘ *Piazza del Carmine, T055-276 8224, www.comune.firenze.it, Wed-Mon 1000-1700, last entry 30 mins before closing, booking essential, €6, time limit 15 mins, max 30 people at a time.*
You walk through peaceful cloisters, then go upstairs to the Brancacci Chapel, a cordoned-off corner of the main church. The extraordinarily dramatic frescoes that cover the walls were commissioned in 1422 by a wealthy merchant, Felice di Michele Brancacci. Now restored, the brilliance of the original colours is stunning. The work was started by Masolino, who had worked with Ghiberti on the doors of the Baptistery and who essentially designed this fresco cycle, which focuses on the life of St Peter. Masolino worked alone for a while, then collaborated with a young artist, Tommaso Cassai, known as Masaccio. When Masolino left the city to work in Budapest, Masaccio continued the work alone, bringing uncompromising emotion to his painting. His panel depicting the *Expulsion of Adam and Eve*, on the left-hand wall, almost screams with their torment – contrast it with Masolino's rather courtly painting of the *Temptation of Adam and Eve* on the opposite wall, in which they look as if they're having a quiet chat under a tree.

Masaccio died aged just 27, and the fresco cycle was eventually completed by Filippino Lippi in 1481-1482. The works that are entirely attributed to Masaccio include *Tribute Money*, next to the *Expulsion*: in this detailed narrative Christ is asked to pay a tax to enter the city of Capernaeum; he points to a fish from whose mouth Saint Peter extracts a coin, with which he pays the tax at the gate. Masaccio also painted *St Peter Healing the Sick with his Shadow* (back wall panel, bottom left): it has a contemporary Florentine setting and many scholars feel it depicts contemporary characters – perhaps Donatello and Masolino.

Basilica di San Miniato al Monte
ⓘ *Via Monte alle Croci, T055-234 2731, Mon-Sat 0800-1200, winter 1500-1800, summer 0800-1900, Sun winter 1500-1800, summer 0800-1900, free, bus 13 from Santa Maria Novella.*
It's well worth making the effort to visit the Church of San Miniato, which sits high above the Arno, overlooking the city. The bus from central Florence takes you up a steep, winding hill to the wide terrace of **piazzale Michelangelo** – a favourite stopping point for coach

Last Suppers in Florence

There are a number of representations of the *Cenacolo* (Last Supper) in Florence. The most famous are Ghirlandaio's versions in San Marco and Ognissanti. But there are lesser-known ones that are worth seeking out. **Sant'Apollonia**, via XVII Aprile, has a 15th-century version by Andrea del Castagno, while **San Salvi**, via San Salvi, (about 30 minutes' walk east of the city centre near the Campo di Marte) has a dramatic 16th-century representation by Andrea del Sarto. The oldest *Last Supper* is Taddeo Gaddi's, now in the museum of **Basilica di Santa Croce** (see page 45). It was painted shortly before the Black Death swept across the city. A 15th-century version in a former monastery, now the **Conservatorio di Foligno**, via Faenza (near the Mercato Centrale), is thought to be the work of Perugino. In the Oltrarno, the 14th-century *Cenacolo* in the **Church of Santo Spirito**, piazza Santo Spirito, was badly damaged in the 18th century. However the one in the complex of **San Giusto della Calza** (piazza della Calza, near the Porta Romana) by Franciabigio is bright and full of action. The building is now a conference centre, but they might let you look in to see it.

tours. Get out here and climb further uphill, and up quite a few steps, and you'll reach this much-loved church, which dates back to the 11th century. It supposedly stands on the spot where St Minias, Florence's first Christian martyr, brought his head after he had been decapitated by Roman persecutors.

A church of the Olivetan order (a branch of the Benedictines), St Miniato has a gleaming white marble façade, inlaid with green marble, which was made in the 11th and 12th centuries. Set in the centre is a rich golden mosaic of *Christ with the Virgin and St Minias*, which practically blazes under the summer sun.

The interior of the church is so full of faded frescoes, carvings and strange symbols that it could easily inspire a *Da Vinci Code*-type novel. The 13th-century floor, or pavement, in the central nave is marble and carved with signs of the zodiac. At the end of the nave is Michelozzo's unusual, freestanding **tabernacle**, embellished with painted panels by Agnolo Gaddi and terracottas by Luca della Robbia. Marble steps lead you up to the choir, where a screen is carved so delicately it looks like lace, and arched high above is another dazzling **Byzantine-style mosaic** of *Christ Pantocrator*. The sacristy is covered in frescoes painted in the 14th century by Spinello Aretino. Down in the crypt are the relics of St Minias. If you're in the church at 1730 in the summer (1630 in winter) you'll be able to hear the monks singing a magical Gregorian chant.

The piazza in front of San Miniato offers wonderful views. It's well worth walking back down into Florence from here – walk downhill, then take the steps on the left (on the other side of the road to the large Il Loggia restaurant). You'll soon come to the **Giardino delle Rose** ⓘ *1 May to mid-Jun, free*, a delightful rose garden where you can lie on the grass and gaze at the distant Duomo. It has to be the city's top summer picnic spot.

Florence listings

For hotel and restaurant price codes and other relevant information, see pages 10-16.

🛏 Where to stay

Around piazza del Duomo *p28,*
map p30

€€€€ Hotel Brunelleschi, piazza Santa Elisabetta 3, off via de' Calzaioli, T055-27370, www.hotelbrunelleschi.it. This hotel, tucked away in a small piazza, cleverly incorporates a former church and a 6th-century watchtower. If you fancy a 'loo with a view', book room 420 – it has a stunning view of the Duomo. The hotel even has its own museum in the basement, where you can see part of a Roman *caldarium*, or hot bath.

€€ Hotel Il Perseo, via dei Cerretani 1, T055-212504, www.hotelperseo.it. Very close to the Duomo, Hotel Perseo takes up 2 floors of an old building (there is a lift). The rooms are light and contemporary, with good, sparkling bathrooms. Modern artworks are dotted around, there's free Wi-Fi access and a selection of books to borrow.

€€ Palazzo Galletti, via Sant'Egidio 12, T055-390 5750, www.palazzogalletti.it. The extremely good-sized rooms at this high quality residence, on the 1st floor of a historic building, are ranged around an internal courtyard. They have high ceilings, good modern bathrooms and flatscreen TVs. There are 11 rooms, 4 of which are suites, and some have lavish frescoes. Breakfast is a buffet downstairs in the former kitchen, which dates back to 1550.

€€ Soggiorno Battistero, piazza San Giovanni 1, T055-295143, www.soggiorno battistero.it. You really can't get much closer to the Duomo than this simple B&B, which has 7 rooms, on the floor above the small Leonardo museum. Some rooms have views. There are no frills and the rooms are simply furnished, but clean. You take breakfast on a tray in your room.

Around piazza della Signoria *p34,*
map p30

€€€€ Gallery Hotel Art, Vicolo dell'Oro 5, T055-27263, www.lungarnocollection.com. With its white sofas and walls, this hotel exudes a determinedly minimalist style. The contemporary art on the walls changes every couple of months, and the restaurant offers Eastern-inspired fusion food. If you really want to treat yourself, go for the Palazzo Vecchio penthouse suite, where there's a terrace with an outdoor bed. (Yes, you get one inside too.)

€€€€ Hotel Continentale, Vicolo dell'Oro 6r, T055-27262, www.lungarnocollection. com. Situated across from the **Gallery Hotel Art**, this hotel is even more self-consciously stylish. The public areas are broken up into separate 'break out' rooms, with white-cushioned seats and chaises longues, and there's a pink and white breakfast bar. There's even a glass lift with banquette seats. Some rooms have views of the Arno, there are white-curtained beds and lots of bleached oak.

€€€€ Residenza d'Epoca in piazza della Signoria, via dei Magazzini 2, T055-239 9546, www.inpiazzadellasignoria.com. A rather chic residence, with 10 rooms and 3 self-catering apartments. The style is uncluttered and traditional with a contemporary twist – the rooms have plasma screen TVs on easels, free Wi-Fi access and modern bathrooms. Breakfast is taken round a long wooden table – though you can ask to have it in your room.

€€€ Hotel Bernini Palace, piazza San Firenze 29, T055-288621, www.hotelbernini. duetorrihotels.com. The location for this plush hotel couldn't be beaten: it's just a 1-min walk from the Uffizi and about 3 mins from Santa Croce, the Duomo and the Ponte Vecchio. Rooms are quiet and comfortable, with gleaming bathrooms. Those on the exclusive Tuscan floor are decorated in Renaissance Florentine style, with beamed ceilings and canopied beds. You breakfast in the frescoed Sala Parlamento – where the Italian parliament met during Florence's spell as capital.

San Marco *p40, maps p26 and p30*

€€€€ Four Seasons, Borgo Pinti 99, T055-26261, www.fourseasons.com/florence. As much a museum as a hotel, the **Four Seasons** is the latest – and most luxurious – addition to the Florentine scene. It comprises 2 Renaissance palaces, which took nearly 8 years to restore, and over 4.5 ha of private gardens: the largest green space in the city. The most stunning rooms are those on the 'noble' floor, adorned with lavish frescoes, chandeliers and silk wall coverings. There's a separate spa with a large gym and a heated outdoor pool. Perfect for honeymooners.

€€€€ Hotel Regency, piazza Massimo d'Azeglio 3, T055-245247, www.regency-hotel.com. On a cool, leafy square just a few blocks from Sant'Ambrogio market is this classy hotel in a 19th-century villa. The atmosphere is friendly and welcoming and there's a lovely courtyard garden – ideal for relaxing in after a hard day's sightseeing. Rooms have large beds and gleaming bathrooms and are well equipped. There's also a private garden suite.

€€€ Hotel Morandi alla Crocetta, via Laura 50, T055-234 4747, www.hotelmorandi.it. This welcoming, family-run hotel is housed in a former convent. Rooms have plenty of historic features – original frescoes in room 29, for example. Bathrooms are a bit small and dated, but the rooms are comfortable, with plasma screen TVs and computers with internet access. Antiques, books and prints are dotted around and it's on a quiet street. It's 1 floor up and there's no lift.

€€ Antica Dimora Johlea, via San Gallo 80, T055-463 3292, www.johanna.it. There's a real home-from-home feel at this classy little B&B. The rooms, decorated in bold colours with antiques and prints, all have 4-poster

beds and plasma screen TVs/DVDs. There is a lovely little terrace, reached by a short flight of stairs, which has stunning views of the Duomo.

€€ Il Guelfo Bianco, via Cavour 29, T055-288330, www.ilguelfobianco.it. Just a couple of mins from the Accademia, this friendly, smallish hotel (40 rooms) has retained plenty of the original features of its 16th-century building. Aperitifs are served each evening in the little bar.

€€ Residenza Johlea, via San Gallo 76, T055-463 3292, www.johanna.it. Part of a small chain run by Lea Gulmanelli and Johanna Vitta, this boutique B&B offers excellent value for money. There are 9 rooms, all stylishly furnished and with private bathrooms in white Carrara marble. There's a table in the hallway where you can help yourself to coffee, tea and fruit.

Self-catering

Residence Hilda, via dei Servi 40, T055-288021, www.residencehilda.it. Slick, modern apartments in the heart of the city: **Residence Hilda** has 12 serviced apartments furnished in crisp, minimalist style, with white walls, wooden floors, sparkling bathrooms and well-equipped kitchens. Excellent value, from €230 per day.

Around San Lorenzo *p43, maps p26 and p30*

€€ Hotel Casci, via Cavour 13, T055-211686, www.hotelcasci.com. The 24 rooms are all different and have flatscreen TVs, DVDs and free Wi-Fi access. There are original frescoes on the ceiling of the breakfast room and a small bar serving drinks and coffees. Many visitors return again.

€ Residenza Johanna 1, via Bonifacio Lupi 14, T055-481896, www.johanna.it. This was the first in the reliable **Johlea & Johanna** chain of chic B&Bs, which really set the standard for stylish and affordable accommodation in Florence. It's a bit hard to find, upstairs in a 19th-century palazzo, but once there you'll find bright rooms with high ceilings, marble or polished wood floors and private bathrooms. You breakfast in your room – they provide you with a basket of goodies.

Santa Croce and around *p45, map p30*
Self-catering
Palazzo Antellesi, piazza Santa Croce 19-22, T055-244456, www.flipkey.com or www.italyperfect.com. This 16th-century palace in the heart of the city offers a taste of grand living. It's divided into 10 apartments (with a further 4 in an annexe), all furnished in different styles, some with original frescoes. Some look on to piazza Santa Croce, while Belvedere has a quiet private terrace. The smallest, Annigoni, sleeps 2 and was the eponymous painter's studio. Minimum stay 6 nights.

Around piazza della Repubblica *p47, map p30*
€€€€ Hotel Savoy, piazza della Repubblica 7, T055-27351, www.hotel savoy.it. For style and luxury in the heart of the city, you can't beat this sleek retreat. Styled by Olga Polizzi, it has spacious contemporary rooms, in shades of cream and oatmeal, marble bathrooms, plasma screen TVs, broadband – all a refreshing change from the ornate gilding that adorns many Italian hotels.
€€€ Antica Torre di Via Tornabuoni 1, via dei Tornabuoni 1, T055-265 8161, www.tornabuoni1.com. Beside the Arno, on one of Florence's smartest streets, is this gorgeous residence in a medieval tower. There are three apartments (with kitchens) and 12 rooms, with TVs, Wi-Fi, marble bathrooms and some private balconies. You can take breakfast on the top-floor terrace, which has glorious views across the city. Room 4 overlooks the river.
€€€ Hotel Beacci Tornabuoni, via dei Tornabuoni 3, T055-212645, www.tornabuonihotels.com. This historic, family-run hotel fills the top floor of a

Renaissance palace. The public rooms have an air of grandeur, with chandeliers, antiques and tapestries. Some of the rooms are decorated with original 18th-century frescoes, and all are slightly different. There's a roof garden where you can have breakfast or drinks.
€€ Hotel Scoti, via dei Tornabuoni 7, T055-292128, www.hotelscoti.com. This welcoming small hotel has just 11 rooms. It's on the 2nd floor of a former palazzo on one of Florence's smartest streets. Inside are *trompe l'oeil* frescoes from the 18th century, tiled floors and comfy chairs. The rooms are simply furnished and overlook a little courtyard. You take breakfast on a tray in your room.

Around piazza Santa Maria Novella *p48, map p30*
€€€€ JK Place, piazza Santa Maria Novella 7, T055 264 5181, www.jkplace.com. This sleek celebrity hideaway has just 20 rooms in an elegant, white-painted townhouse opposite Santa Maria Novella Church. Bedrooms are super-stylish, with large mirrors and gleaming bathrooms – one has a bath in which you can sit and look over to the Duomo.

The Oltrarno *p49, map p26*
€€€€ Palazzo Magnani Feroni, borgo San Frediano 5, T055-239 9544, www.palazzomagnaniferoni.com or www.florencepalace.it. An elegant residence in a 16th-century palace in the Oltrarno. There are 12 suites, all furnished with antiques and works of art from the owners' collection. The smallest suite's walls are covered in frescoes. All bathrooms are stocked with Bulgari products, and public rooms have Murano glass chandeliers and flowers. The top-floor terrace has views of the Duomo and Campanile.

Camping
Camping Michelangelo, viale Michelangelo 80, T055-681 1977, www.ecvacanze.it.

There are great views over the city from this campsite close to piazzale Michelangelo and the glorious Church of San Miniato al Monte. You can rent a tent and there are pitches for campervans and caravans. There's a shop, bar and internet access.

℗ Restaurants

Around piazza del Duomo *p28, map p30*

€€€ Angels, via del Proconsolo 29/31, T055-239 8762, www.ristoranteangels.it. Daily 1200-1500, 1930-2300. Trendy but pricy candlelit restaurant situated in a historic building. During the winter there's a piano bar that serves a wide range of cocktails from 1800. Dishes might include seafood risotto with saffron, home-made pasta with squid, or baked sea bass.

€ Cantinetta dei Verrazzano, via dei Tavolini 18/20r, T055-268590. Mon-Sat 0800-2100. This *cantinetta* functions as a deli/café and is a great place for a quick lunch. Join locals for a plate of cheeses, cold meats, breads and wine from the *cantinetta's* own vineyards. There are a few seats in one corner, as well as a wooden bench where you can perch. An ideal place to pick up picnic supplies.

€ Da Vinattieri, via Santa Margherita 6r. 1000-0100 (can vary). The sign reads "*Trippa e Lampredotto*" and there are few places like this left in Florence. Just a hole in the wall, a counter with a couple of stools outside and a chance to sample the local speciality: tripe. Panini with tripe is one option, while *lampredotto* (cow's stomach) is another. Do as the regulars do and wash it down with red wine.

Cafés and bars

Bar Gallo, piazza Duomo 1r, T055-219251, www.b-gallo.it. Daily 0800-0100 (sometimes closed Tue). This funky bar/lounge attracts everyone, from young Florentines out for cocktails to tired tourists taking a break. Just by the Baptistery, it has a contemporary interior, seats outside and a room upstairs where the likes of Gucci hold exclusive gatherings. The menu offers everything from crêpes with Nutella to steaks. Come early evening for an aperitif or at lunchtime for a sandwich.

Grom, via del Campanile 4, T055-216158. Daily Apr-Sep 1030-2400, Oct-Mar 1030-2300. Tucked away on the corner of a back street, just a couple of minutes from the Duomo, **Grom**, say locals, has the best ice cream in Florence. And it really is superb: no artificial colourings or additives, organic eggs, rich cream. You can have a cone for a few euros – a scoop of extra dark chocolate, plus one of milk and mint, makes a winning combo. There are a few seats inside.

Around piazza della Signoria *p34, map p30*

€€€ Gustavino, via della Condotta 37r, T055-239 9806, www.gustavino.it. Daily 1900-1130, also Sat-Sun 1230-1530. Sophisticated **Gustavino**, with its silvery chairs, high arched ceilings and glass-fronted kitchen, attracts a fashionable crowd, who come for Tuscan food with a modern twist. The menu might feature home-made *pici* pasta with guinea fowl ragù spiced with chocolate and Parmesan cheese, and beef fillet with onion marmalade. The wine list features wines from the family's own estate.

€€ La Canova di Gustavino, via della Condotta 29, T055-239 9806, www. gustavino.it. Daily 1200-2400. Situated next door to its sister restaurant **Gustavino**, **La Canova** has a cosier, more traditional atmosphere and serves classic Tuscan dishes, many of which require longer, slower cooking. As well as dishes such as *ossobuco* in tomato sauce, you can also find light lunch options such as Tuscan bread with lardo and honey, and Cinta Senese cold cuts.

€ 'Ino, via dei Georgofili 3r/7r, T055-219208, www.ino-firenze.com. Mon-Sat 1100-2000, Sun 1200-1700. Tucked away near the Uffizi is this lovely little wine and sandwich bar. You can sit inside and have wine and a tasting plate of fresh cheeses and meats, and they'll also make up panini for you to take away. Worth seeking out when you want lunch on the run, or picnic supplies.

Cafés and bars
Gelateria dei Neri, via dei Neri 20/22r, T055-210034. Daily 1100-2400 (may be shorter hours in winter). Handmade ice creams in enticing flavours such as pistachio and chilli or strawberry pie – there are even soy and yoghurt versions too. It's in a back street between the Palazzo Vecchio and piazza Santa Croce, and a favourite with locals.
Rivoire, piazza della Signoria 4r, T055-214412, www.rivoire.it. Tue-Sat 0730-2400. OK, you can spend over €5 on a coffee here, but **Rivoire**, which dates back to 1872, is a Florentine institution. Seats on the outdoor terrace offer peerless views of the Palazzo Vecchio and it's a great place just to sit and soak up the city's atmosphere. In winter, snuggle inside with a hot chocolate and admire the grand turn-of-the-century interior.

San Marco *p40, maps p26 and p30*
€€€ Cibrèo, via Andrea del Verrocchio 8r, T055-234 1100, www.edizioniteatrodel salecibreofirenze.it. Tue-Sat 1250-1430, 1900-2315, closed Aug. Situated right beside Sant'Ambrogio market, **Cibrèo** is a long-established Florentine restaurant serving sophisticated versions of classic Tuscan dishes. On the opposite corner is **Cibrèo Caffè**, which offers the same dishes in a less formal setting. Nearby Teatro del Sale (via de' Macci 111r) is a private members' club under the same ownership. Join as a non-resident, then have access to their buffet breakfasts and lunches, as well as their dinner buffets, which are followed by performances.

Around San Lorenzo *p43, map p26*
€€€ Taverna del Bronzino, via delle Ruote 27r, T055-495220, www.tavernadel bronzino.com. Mon-Sat 1230-1400, 1930-2200, closed 3 weeks in Aug. This restaurant is the sort of place that's popularly described

as 'fine dining'. Behind a huge wooden door you'll find an air of calm, with tables set under a white canopy, cream linen tablecloths and deep green seats. Dishes tend towards Italian classics, with *primi* such as creamy risotto with ricotta and spinach, and *secondi* such as *ossobuco* with rice and saffron.
€€ Osteria Pepo, via Rosina 6r, T055-283259, www.pepo.it. Daily 1230-1430, 1900-2230, closed Sun in summer. This relaxed *osteria* is just off the bustling Central Market. It has an informal, rustic feel at lunchtime – then morphs into something more sophisticated at night, with candles and crisp white tablecloths. Food and wine are Tuscan, and offer good value.

Santa Croce and around *p45, maps p26 and p30*
€€€ Gastone, via Matteo Palmieri 26r, T055-263 8763, www.gastonefirenze.it. Mon-Sat 1200-1500, 1900-2300, bar open Mon-Sat 1100-2400. Trendy **Gastone** is quite a favourite with locals. The décor is light and bright, with blue-painted wooden floors and prints on the walls. It's a great place for pre-dinner drinks, or a post-sightseeing pick-me-up. The menu changes twice a month and features dishes such as fish ravioli, sea bass or duck breast with berries. Wines featured come from across Tuscany.
€€ Acqua al 2, via della Vigna Vecchia 40r, T055-284170, www.acquaal2.it. Daily 1930-0100. Close to the Teatro Verdi, the walls of this restaurant are hung with plates signed by performers. It can get extremely busy. The longish menu ranges from pastas to steaks, with some dishes appearing on a seasonal basis.
€€ Il Pizzaiuolo, via de' Macci 113r, T055-241171. Mon-Sat 1230-1415, 1930-2400. This busy pizzeria is close to Sant'Ambrogio market and offers a wide range of pizzas, cooked in a wood oven. You might have to queue and share a table – both locals and tourists come here, and service can be brusque.

€ **Bistrot Baldoria**, borgo Allegri 4r/via San Giuseppe 18r, T055-234 7220. Daily 1100-1600, 1830-2400. This friendly trattoria attracts plenty of locals, and there are a few tables squeezed on to the street outside. Come for large plates of sheep's cheese with pears and nuts, home-made pasta and a wide selection of Tuscan wines. Unusually for Florence, there's no cover charge.

€ **Osteria del Caffè Italiano**, via Isola delle Stinche 11/13r, T055-289368, www.caffeitaliano.it. Tue-Sun 1230-1430, 1930 till late. You could easily walk straight past this little pizzeria, which adjoins the **Caffè Italiano** restaurant. However, it does some of the best pizzas in the city – made in a, wood-fired oven. There are only 4 tables and you have a choice of just 3 toppings – but they're delicious and made with fresh ingredients. Gets busy with queues for takeaways.

Cafés and bars
Il Gelato Vivoli, via Isola delle Stinche 7, T055-292334. Closed Mon. **Vivoli** is the most famous *gelateria* in Florence, dating back to 1929 – many guidebooks claim it's also the best. There are always queues of tourists, scooping up spoonfuls of ice cream from little tubs – you don't get cones here.

Note di Vino, borgo de' Greci 4/6r, T055-218750, www.notedivino.it. There's not much more than a hole in the wall and a small counter at this busy *enoteca*. Everyone sits at the wooden tables lined along the street outside, and there's a selection of aperitifs early in the evening. Wines include Tuscan classics such as Brunello di Montalcino and sparkling prosecco.

Oibò, borgo de' Greci 1/1a, T055-263 8611, www.oibo.net. Daily 0800-0200. **Oibò** functions as a café during the day and a lively cocktail bar after 1900. The bar is all lit up in blue, there's loud music and a small seating area upstairs. Try a *copa gabana* – a mix of gin, bitter orange and apricot brandy.

Around piazza della Repubblica *p47, map p30*
€€€ **L'Incontro**, piazza della Repubblica 7, T055-27351, www.hotelsavoy.it. Daily 1230-1500, 1930-2230. Soft music, contemporary art and modern Tuscan food make **L'Incontro** a stylish dining option. It's the restaurant of the **Hotel Savoy** and a place to see and be seen. Come at lunchtime, nibble on a Caesar salad or some artichoke and saffron risotto, and watch the crowds strolling around the piazza. Booking advised in the evening.

€€€ **Rossini**, Lungarno Corsini 4, T055-239 9224, www.ristoranterossini.it. Thu-Tue 1230-1430, 1930-2230. Gourmet food on the Arno: this restaurant, in a former palazzo, is the place to come for a treat. Under the high arched ceiling you can work your way through a 6-course €100 tasting menu. If you blanch at that price, the 2-course 'light lunch' is €35 including wine and coffee. The cellar contains around 600 wines, from all over Italy.

€€ **Mangiafoco Caffè**, borgo Santissimi Apostoli 26r, T055-265 8170. Mon-Sat 0900-2130. This is as much a wine bar as a café. Have a light lunch such as bruschetta, or go for a tasting plate of Tuscan cheeses and cured meats. Come in the early evening for aperitifs and you can help yourself to the free buffet and snacks.

€ **Mariano**, via del Parione 19r, T055-214067. This popular bar gets packed with locals at lunchtime. Panini are freshly made in front of you, crammed with salads and cured meats. There are also a few seats (if you can find one). It's a great choice for a takeaway lunch, though you will have to fight for attention.

Cafés and bars
Caffè Florian, via del Parione 28r, T055-284291, www.caffeflorian.com. Mon-Thu 0830-1930, Fri-Sat 0830-2000. This is a Florentine outpost of the famous Florian in Venice. Tucked away in a back street near the Arno, it's a small but chic retreat. As well

as serving coffees it also sells chocolates, pastries, jams and liqueurs.

Gilli, piazza della Repubblica 39r, T055-213896, www.gilli.it. Wed-Mon 0700-0100. Once a meeting place for artists and writers, Gilli now attracts everyone from tourists to well-heeled locals. It's one of the grand old cafés of Florence, with a marble bar, lots of dark polished wood and mirrors.

Giubbe Rosse, piazza della Repubblica 13/14r, T055-212280, www.giubberosse.it. Daily 0830-0200. There's an air of faded grandeur about this historic café. Founded in the 19th century, it was once a meeting place for the German community, and later became a favourite haunt of Florence's literati. Today there are arty prints on the walls, lots of dark wood fittings and seats out on the piazza.

La Rinascente Caffè, piazza della Repubblica 1, T055-219113, www.rinascente.it. Mon-Sat 1000-2000, Sun 1030-1900. Who cares about the coffee with views like this? This café, on the 5th floor of **La Rinascente** department store, has an outdoor terrace with mesmerizing views of the Duomo (so close you feel you could almost touch it). Come for coffee or an early evening glass of wine.

Around piazza Santa Maria Novella
p48, maps p26 and p30

€€€ Cantinetta Antinori, piazza degli Antinori 3, T055-292234, www.cantinetta-antinori.com or www.antinori.it. Mon-Fri 1230-1430, 1930-2230. Set inside the courtyard of an old palazzo, with just a discreet wooden sign outside, this *cantinetta* simply oozes wealth. Inside are sharp-suited staff, shiny wooden tables and cream walls. Dishes range from delicious fillet of fresh turbot to pasta with mussels and fresh white beans.

€€€ Il Latini, via dei Palchetti 6r, T055-210916, www.illatini.com. Tue-Sun 1230-1430, 1930-2230, closed Mon. Locals consistently mention this as one of their favourite restaurants. It's family run and has a rustic, Tuscan look, with hams hanging

from the ceiling and black and white photos on the walls. The food is similarly Tuscan, and it's the place to try meaty dishes such as *trippa alla fiorentina* and roast lamb. It gets busy, so it's best to book.

€ Caffè San Carlo, borgo Ognissanti 32/34r, T055-216879, www.caffesancarlo.com. Mon-Sat 0730-2400. A cheerful, friendly café: contemporary red and white colour scheme, seats outside on the street, and glasses of wine. Come for fast panini at lunchtime or pasta in the evening. They also serve aperitifs and cocktails.

€ La Dantesca, via Panzani 57r, T055-212287. Daily 1200-1500, 1830-2330. No frills at this place near the railway station. It has pink-washed walls, a TV set above the door, a large wood-fired oven, and busy staff serving delicious thin and crispy pizzas, which many locals reckon are some of the best in the city. Other dishes include Florentine fried rabbit, or gnocchetti with Gorgonzola.

The Oltrarno *p49, maps p26 and p30*

€€€ Borgo San Jacopo, borgo San Jacopo 62r, T055-281661, www.lungarnohotels.com. Wed-Mon 1930-2400. Style-conscious dining at the **Lungarno Hotels**' restaurant on the Arno. You might find first courses such as gnocchi with quail sauce, and mains such as fillet of beef with asparagus. The most highly prized tables are those on the little terrace, right on the river – there are only 4, so book early if you want one.

€€€ Enoteca le Barrique, via del Leone 40r, near piazza del Carmine, T055-224192, www.enotecalebarrique.com. Tue-Sun evenings. Light wood tables, high ceilings and relaxed dining at this trendy *enoteca*. The menu isn't divided into courses – choose whatever you want, whether it's fresh pasta with herbs, pumpkin ravioli or squid with cannellini beans.

€€€ Filipepe, via San Niccolò 39r, T055-200 1397, www.filipepe.com. Daily 1900-2400. This place has a quirky, theatrical feel, the food is modern Italian, and fish is a speciality. You might find salt cod with chickpea and pistachio mousse; pasta with sardines, fennel and pine nuts; and monkfish with courgettes, apples and capers.

€€€ Olio & Convivium, via di Santo Spirito 4, T055-265 8198, www.convivium firenze.com. Tue-Sat 1000-1500, 1800-2230, Mon 1000-1500. A deli with a difference, the upmarket shop stocks all sorts of gourmet Tuscan foods from ham to olive oil, but also has dining tables. Tasting plates, which include wine and dessert, are worth trying. Check out the daily specials, which can range from risottos to home-made pasta with monkfish and tomatoes.

€€ Borgo Antico, piazza Santo Spirito 6r, T055-210437, www.borgoanticofirenze.com. Daily 1200-2400. Convenient if you've been to the Pitti Palace, this popular trattoria attracts a lively mix of young locals and tourists. There are plenty of seats on the piazza, and it's a place for relaxed dining – wooden tables, paper placemats and drinks in tumblers. Come for pizzas, or hearty dishes such as gnocchi with blue cheese and chicory or salt cod with chickpeas.

€€ Rifrullo, via San Niccolò 55r, T055-234 2621, www.ilrifrullo.com. Daily 0700-0100, may close for 2 weeks in Aug. This café/ restaurant/wine bar is a long-established favourite. It always seems busy, but it has a pleasantly laid-back atmosphere and a pretty garden at the back. Come for coffee, a quick lunch or a more substantial evening meal, such as sea bass with tomato and olive sauce or beef fillet with green pepper sauce. Aperitifs are served from 1900: for a few euros you can have a drink and help yourself to the buffet.

€ Antica Porta, via Senese 23r, T055-220527. Tue-Sun 1930-2400. This simple pizzeria, just outside the Porta Romana, is a favourite with local diners. The pizzas are made in a traditional wood-fired oven, and home-made pasta dishes are posted on a daily blackboard menu. Desserts, like tiramisù, are freshly made too.

Cafés and bars
Il Panino del Chianti, via de' Bardi 63r, T055-239 8831. Daily 1045-2130 (longer at weekends). Just beside the Ponte Vecchio, this tiny bar/*enoteca* has just 1 table, and a good choice of Tuscan wines that you can purchase by the glass. You can also get panini, and there are aperitifs after 1800.

Le Volpi e l'Uva, piazza dei Rossi 1, T055-239 8132, www.levolpieluva.com. Mon-Sat 1100-2100. This busy *enoteca* attracts a loyal following. It should be on any wine lover's itinerary, as they stock a wide range of little-known wines, sourced from small producers across Italy. You can enjoy local cheeses and meats while you're there.

⏻ Entertainment

Florence *p24, maps p26 and p30*
For listings of concerts, films and other events, buy *Firenze Spettacolo* (www.firenze spettacolo.it) or the English-language paper *The Florentine* (www.theflorentine.net).

Children
Children are widely welcomed in Florence, and state museums offer free admission to under-18s, but they can quickly get bored if overloaded with visits to cultural sights. The best child-centred tours are at the Palazzo Vecchio, where tours run by costumed guides really help to bring the palace alive. They're run by the **Associazione Musei dei Ragazzi** (T055-276 8224, www.museiragazzifirenze.it) based in the palace, which also offers some visits to other attractions, such as the Brancacci Chapel.

Older ones should enjoy the challenge of climbing to the top of the Duomo or the Campanile, and the Boboli Gardens and Parco delle Cascine (west of the city centre, bus 17) offer them a chance to let off steam. Football fans will welcome a trip outside the city centre to the **Museo del Calcio** (viale Aldo Palazzeschi 20, Coverciano, T055-600526, www.museodelcalcio.it, Mon-Fri 0900-1300, 1600-1800, Sat 0900-1300, €3/€1.50, bus 17).

Cinema
Goldoni, via Serragli 109, T055-222437. Around €7. Shows original language films on Wed or Thu.
Odeon Cinehall, piazza Strozzi 2, T055-295051, www.cinehall.it. Closed Aug. Around €7.20. Shows original language films on Mon and Tue.

Clubs
If you love aperitifs and a cool Italian crowd, there are a couple of bars/clubs that should hit the spot.
Central Park, via Fosso Macinante 2, Parco delle Cascine, T055-333505. Entry around €20-25. A popular commercial summer dance venue, with outdoor dancefloors.
Colle Bereto, piazza Strozzi, T055-283156. An über-trendy place with a designer-clad 30-something crowd with cash to flash. There's a VIP area and a very plush terrace.
Girasol, via del Romito 1, T055-474948, www.girasol.it. Out by the Fortezza, this is a popular and lively Latin bar with plenty of live music.
Noir, lungarno Corsini, T055-210751. Has a great view of the Ponte Vecchio and a 20/30-something, well-dressed crowd. Come for a Martini at aperitif time and stay to dance.
Tenax, via Pratese 46, nr Peretola Airport, T055-308160, www.tenax.org. Thu-Sat, closed in summer, entry from €20 on Sat. Bus 29 or 30 (or get a taxi). Lively place that doubles as a club and live-music venue. Noted for its famous DJs, and great dance floor. Attracts international acts. Thu is student night, disco on Fri and cool clubbing on Sat.
Universale Firenze, via Pisana 77r, Oltrarno, T055-221122, www.universalefirenze.it. Thu-Sun, closed Jun-Sep. Trendy dance venue in a flashily converted cinema, with a large bar, sweeping staircase and restaurants and clubbing area.
YAB, via dei Sassetti 5r, T055-21560, www.yab.it. Oct-May Mon-Sat, restaurant Thu-Sat 2100-2300, entry around €15, meal/disco

€25. Long-established glamorous club with a sheeny disco feel. There's a restaurant, lots of mirrors and a huge dance floor. Mon is hip-hop night and attracts a lively 20-something crowd; Fri is house.

Music, theatre and dance
Jazz Club, via Nuova de' Caccini 3, off Borgo Pinti, T055-247 9700, www.jazzclubfirenze.com. Tue-Sat from 2100, membership (join at door) €5. Long-established jazz venue that attracts acts on the up, and those at the top. Big names like Joe Diorio, Marco Tamburini and Sandro Gibellini have all appeared here. It attracts a knowledgeable crowd, many coming for the Tue/Wed jam sessions, and has a laid-back atmosphere and food and wine.
Mandela Forum, viale Pasquale Paoli 3, T055-678841, www.mandelaforum.it. East of the city centre – take bus 17, 10 or 20. Major venue for big-name international acts.
Teatro Communale, corso Italia 16, T055-277 9350, www.maggiofiorentino.com. The city's main performance space, and home to its orchestra, L'Orchestra del Maggio Musicale Fiorentino. The Teatro del Maggio Musicale Fiorentino puts on concerts here throughout the year, as well as the summer festival.
Teatro della Pergola, via della Pergola, T055-226 4353, www.pergola.firenze.it. Lovely old theatre staging classic productions, plus some opera and chamber music.
Teatro Verdi, via Ghibellina 99, T055-212320, www.teatroverdifirenze.it. This large theatre hosts musicals, dance and music concerts.

☉ Shopping

Florence *p24, maps p26 and p30*
Art and antiques
Galleria Romanelli, Borgo San Frediano 70, T055-239 6047, www.raffaelloromanelli.com. Mon afternoon and Tue-Sat 0900-1900. This studio in the Oltrarno is crammed with marble, bronze and plaster sculptures, giving

it the look of a small museum. 6 generations of the same family have worked here and the pride they take in their work is evident. They'll take on commissions, and have a workshop on site.

L'Ippogrifo, via Santo Spirito 5r, T055-213255, www.stampeippogrifo.com. Mon-Sat 1000-1900, closed Sat in summer. Husband-and-wife team Gianni Raffaelli and Francesca Bellesi, have worked here in their studio in the Oltrarno for over 10 years. They create delicate, handmade etchings using traditional techniques and will take on commissions too. You can watch them working in the studio, though it's best to call in advance to check.

Pietra di Luna, via Maggio 4, T055-265 8257, www.biancobianchi.com. Tue-Sat 1000-1300, 1530-1930. One of the fascinating traditional crafts of the Oltrarno is *scagliola* – a decorative technique that was once used to imitate marble and the costly inlaid work known as *pietra dura*. The Bianchi family have revived the art: mixtures of moonstone dust, dyes and glue are etched into stone, moonstone or marble to create brightly coloured patterns. You'll find full-sized tables as well as inlaid boxes and paperweights – and you might sometimes see someone demonstrating the art.

Books and stationery

Abacus, via de' Ginori 28r, T055-219719, www.abacusfirenze.it. Mon 1500-1900, Tue-Fri 0930-1330, 1400-1930, Sat 0930-1345, 1500-1900. As well as being bookbinders and restorers, working with fine leather, **Abacus** also stock items such as leather-bound address books and photo albums, which make great gifts. Their workshop is next to their shop.

Giulio Giannini & Figlio, piazza de' Pitti 37r, T055-212621, www.giuliogiannini.it. Daily 1000-1900. The Giannini family have been working as bookbinders in this part of Florence since 1856. They also make marbled paper and stationery items. Their workshop, tucked away in the Oltrarno by

the Pitti Palace, is worth a visit. Call first to check it's convenient.

Paperback Exchange, via delle Oche 4r, T055 293460, www.papex.it. Mon-Fri 0900-1930, Sat 1030-1930. This English-language bookshop is a great place to pick up translations of Italian titles, as well as all sorts of new and used books with an Italian theme. If you forgot to bring your copy of *A Room with a View*, here's where you'll find it. The friendly chap behind the counter also seems to do a great line in giving directions to bewildered tourists.

R Vannucchi, via Condotta 26/28r, T055-216752. Mon-Sat 1000-1930. Florence is famous for its handmade paper, and it makes a great gift to take home. The paper here is some of the best – and you'll also find greetings cards and other stationery, pens, and leather wallets and diaries.

Clothing and shoes

Antonio Gatto, piazza de' Pitti 5, T055-294725. Tue-Sun 0900-1900, Mon afternoon. Antonio is a tailor and former costume designer. Here, in his shop in the Oltrarno, he makes clothes for both men and women. You can buy off the peg or have something made to measure. He also makes a wide selection of women's hats.

Ceri Vintage, via dei Serragli 26r, T055-217978. Mon 1530-1930, Tue-Sat 1000-1230, 1530-1930. Dressing-up heaven at this store in the Oltrarno, which sells men's and women's vintage clothes and accessories. Items date back to the 19th century and up to the 1980s. They also stock a few new lines from Denmark.

Grevi, via della Spada 11/13r, T055-264139, www.grevi.com. Mon-Sat 1000-1300, 1400-2000. You'll find hats galore at this specialist shop near piazza Santa Maria Novella. There are handmade ladies' hats in a huge range of styles, and gloves as well if you want to match.

Stefano Bemer, Borgo San Frediano 143r, T055-222558, www.stefanobemer.it. Mon-Fri 0900-1300, 1500-1930, Sat 0900-1300. Tucked away in the Oltrarno is this specialist shoe shop, selling made-to-measure shoes – mainly for men, but with some styles for women. You'll need to return 2-3 months after your 1st visit to have a fitting. It will cost around €300 to have a last made, then €1800 for a pair of men's shoes, €1500 for ladies. The price, you'll be glad to hear, does fall if you order more.

Food and drink
Bacco Nudo, via de' Macci 59/61r, T055-243298, www.bacconudo.it. Mon-Sat 0900-1315, 1600-2015. Close to Sant'Ambrogio market, this shop has a wide selection of Tuscan wines, as well as the best-known Italian wines and grappa. Some wines are available from vats – they'll fill up a bottle for you. They also do tastings.
Dolcissima, via Maggio 61r, T055-239 6268. Tue-Sat 0800-2000, Sun 0900-1400. This *pasticceria* in the Oltrarno sells a selection of cakes, chocolates and croissants.
La Buca del Vino, via Romana 129r, T055-233 5021, www.labucadelvino.it. Mon 1600-2000, Tue-Sat 1000-1330, 1600-2000. This wine and oil shop in the Oltrarno offers an introduction to wines from selected small-scale producers in Tuscany. Come in and taste the wine, then watch as they fill up a bottle for you from one of the huge barrels. It's an inexpensive way of purchasing wine – they'll ship some home if you wish. The olive oils they sell are also high quality.

Jewellery
Amber Line, piazza de' Pitti 6, T055-288519. Mon-Sat 1000-1800, Sun 1100-1900. This shop opposite the Pitti Palace sells a wide range of amber jewellery. The amber, from Russia and Scandinavia, comes in many colours including deep red and even green.
Penko, via Ferdinando Zannetti 14-16r, T055-211661, www.penkofirenze.it. Tue-Sat 0900-2100 (but closed Sat afternoon in Jul), Mon afternoon. There's a long tradition of handmade gold jewellery in Florence, and Paolo Penko keeps the craft alive in his workshop near the Duomo. He

makes reproductions of famous pieces of jewellery and old designs, and will take on commissions. You can ask for a demo – he's often working away in the shop.

Markets
Cascine, viale Lincoln, Parco delle Cascine. Tue 0800-1300. On the edge of the city centre, this weekly market sells everything from clothes to food.
Mercato Centrale, piazza Mercato Centrale. Mon-Sat 0700-1400 and Sat afternoon in winter. The city's largest permanent food market is lively and colourful. Whether you're looking for fruit, fish, cheese or meat, you should find it here.
Mercato delle Pulci, piazza dei Ciompi. Summer daily 0900-2000, winter Tue-Sun 0900-1930. You can hunt for a variety of antiques and bric-a-brac in this small flea market, which grows much larger on the last Sunday of each month when the stalls extend down the side streets around the piazza.
Mercato Nuovo, off via Porta Rossa. Summer daily 0900-2000, winter Tue-Sun 0900-1930. Always crammed with visitors having their photos taken rubbing the nose of *Il Porcellino*, the bronze wild boar, Mercato Nuovo is essentially an accessories market selling bags, scarves and wallets.
San Lorenzo, piazza San Lorenzo and around. Summer daily 0900-2000, winter Tue-Sun 0900-1930. Leather market selling items such as bags, belts and souvenirs.
Sant'Ambrogio, piazza Ghiberti, Mon-Sat 0700-1400. Fabulous fruit and vegetables, along with a few stalls selling cheese, bread and oils. This is a real locals' market and the produce is excellent.

Pharmacies
Bizzarri, via Condotta 32r, T055-211580, www.bizzarri-fi.biz. Tue-Sat 0930-1300, 1500-1930. Florence has a number of historic herbalists and this one is fascinating. It dates back to 1842 and has lovely old wooden cabinets, which contain everything from herbal remedies to linseed oil. Cash only.

Officina Profumo-Farmaceutica di Santa Maria Novella, via della Scala 16, T055-216276, www.smnovella.com. Daily 0900-2000. This historic pharmacy was founded in the 13th century, turning medicinal herbs into remedies. It opened to the public in 1612. Inside are dark wooden display cases, ceramic storage jars and 14th-century frescoes. You can buy elixirs, pot-pourri, soaps and candles.

✪ What to do

Florence *p24, maps p26 and p30*
Cultural tours
Isango (UK), T+44 (0) 203-355 1240, www.isango.com. They offer a range of guided tours and cultural experiences in Florence and Tuscany, ranging from a Segway tour of the city centre to a cheese and wine tasting tour. You can also have excellent private guided tours, such as one of Chianti and the Tuscan hill towns. They can also arrange cookery courses.

Cycling
Florence By Bike, via San Zanobi 120r, T055-488992, www.florencebybike.it. An established bike rental company (you can hire city bikes by the hour), it also suggests self-guided tours and offers a guided Chianti Bike Tour for around €70. **I Bike Italy**, T347-638 3976, www.ibike italy.com. They offer 1- and 2-day cycling tours of Tuscany: the 2-day tour goes from Florence to Siena.

Golf
Circolo del Golf dell'Ugolino, via Chiantigiana 3, Grassina, T055-230 1009, www.golfugolino.it. About 20 mins' drive from central Florence (take the SP222 past Grassina). This is an 18-hole course (green fee €70). It's not always open to non-members, so check in advance and reserve a tee-time.

Walking
Artviva, via dei Sassetti 1, T055-264 5033, www.italy.artviva.com. This established company offers a wide range of walking and cycling tours. Their Original Florence Walk lasts 3 hrs.

⊖ Transport

Florence *p24, maps p26 and p30*
Regular trains to **Pisa** (1 hr 5 mins), **Pistoia** (40 mins), **Arezzo** (45-90 mins). To reach **Grosseto**, travel via Pisa or Livorno (2 hrs 53 mins). Regular buses to **Siena** (1 hr 15 mins), also buses to **Volterra** (1 hr 10 mins).

❶ Directory

Florence *p24, maps p26 and p30*
ATMs Via PS Maria and other cash points around piazza della Signoria and piazza della Repubblica. **Pharmacies** 24-hr pharmacies at Santa Maria Novella station concourse, also Molteni, via Calzaiuoli 7r and All'Insegna del Moro, piazza S Giovanni. **Hospital** Main hospital at Policlinico di Careggi, viale Morgagni 85. Outside the city centre **University Hospital Careggi**, Largo G A Brambilla, 3, T055-794111. Also Santa Maria Nuova, piazza S. Maria Nuova.

Fiesole and the Mugello

For centuries Fiesole has been regarded as a leafy retreat from Florence, and it still serves that purpose today. Just 20 minutes from Florence (take bus 7 from Santa Maria Novella) it has a pleasant 'village' atmosphere, interesting sights and famously fabulous views of Florence itself.

Arriving in Fiesole and the Mugello
Tourist information Fiesole's tourist information office is at via Portigiani 3, T055-598720/597 8373, www.comune.fiesole.fi.it.

Fiesole
Fiesole was an Etruscan settlement (you can see the remains of the Etruscan wall, which is made up of blocks of stone so enormous it's difficult to imagine how they ever moved them). It was later settled by the Romans, who built a 3000-seat **theatre** ① *summer daily 0930-1900, Mar-Oct 0930-1800, winter Wed-Mon 0930-1700, €5*, which you can still see. The main square is **piazza Mino**, surrounded by nice little shops and cafés and dominated by the **Duomo**, which dates back to the 11th century. The artist Fra Angelico entered monastic life when he joined the monastery of **San Domenico in Fiesole** ① *T055-59230, www.sandomenicodifiesole.op.org*. There's a work by him in the church of San Domenico and another in the chapterhouse of the monastery. Just outside the town is one of Tuscany's swankiest hotels, the **Villa San Michele** (www.villasanmichele.com) – a former monastery set in its own grounds. If your budget doesn't run to staying there, you could always treat yourself to lunch instead.

The Mugello
You could happily spend the day in Fiesole. But if you've got a car, you could use it as the starting point for a tour of the **Mugello**, a gorgeous corner of Tuscany characterized by fertile valleys, wooded hills and pretty hamlets – and barely explored by tourists. Drive north to **San Piero a Sieve**, where there's an 11th-century church with a font by Luca della Robbia. The Mugello was the ancestral home of the Medici, who used the area as a hunting ground, and they've left their mark everywhere. You can follow a walking trail from San Piero a Sieve to see **Trebbio Castle**, commissioned by Cosimo I (open to groups only), while another trail leads to the **Fortress of San Martino**, also built by the Medici and currently being restored. You could also visit the **Bosco ai Frati Convent** (open daily), which dates back to the 11th century. In its small museum is a crucifix attributed to Donatello.

If you now drive east you'll reach **Borgo San Lorenzo**, the main town in the region, where the Romanesque parish church contains a 13th-century Madonna attributed to Giotto. If you love fine ceramics, visit the **Chini Ceramic Museum** (www.villapecori.it) on the edge of the town. Housed in the elegant Villa Pecori Giraldi, it contains ceramics produced by the local Chini ceramic factory, as well as artworks by Pietro Annigoni.

Not far from Borgo San Lorenzo is **Colle di Vespignano**, Vicchio, where Giotto was born. The house, which is traditionally known as his birthplace, has been turned into a

museum ⓘ *T055-843 9225, www.casadigiotto.com, Thu-Fri 1000-1300, Sat-Sun 1000-1300, 1500-1900, closed during the week Oct-May.* Vasari has it that Cimabue was walking in the Mugello when he met a young shepherd – Giotto – drawing on a stone and encouraged him to move to Florence.

A short drive further east you'll reach **Vicchio**, the birthplace of Fra Angelico. From here you can follow the course of the Sieve River, past Dicomano and on to **Rufina**. This is wine country, where you can stop off for tours and tastings of wines as well as olive oils. You can also visit the **Vine and Wine Museum** at Rufina (www.villapoggioreale.it) before driving back to Florence.

Fiesole and the Mugello listings

For hotel and restaurant price codes and other relevant information, see pages 10-16.

● Where to stay

€€€ Villa Campestri, via di Campestri 19/22, Vicchio di Mugello, T055-849 0107, www.villacampestri.it. This tastefully restored villa 38 km northeast of Florence is a real treat. It dates back to the 13th century and belonged to an aristocratic Florentine family for over 700 years. The present owner bought it from them and has retained its original features: you feel as if you're staying in a Renaissance palace. There are extensive grounds, an excellent restaurant and an oleoteca where you can do tutored olive oil tastings.

€€ Casa Palmira, via Faentina, Località Feriolo, Polcanto, T055-840 9749, www. casapalmira.it. Set in quiet countryside just 9 km from Fiesole and 16 km from Florence, this is the friendliest B&B imaginable. Assunta and Stefano make you feel immediately welcome, helping you with your luggage, offering you drinks and showing you their pretty garden and swimming pool. Guests can make themselves hot drinks in the large kitchen/dining room and relax by the log fire on chilly nights. They'll make you dinner if you ask in advance – lovely Tuscan food. They have many repeat visitors, so book well ahead. No credit cards.

Pisa

Pisa is now synonymous with just one thing: the Leaning Tower. Yet in medieval times it was a powerful maritime republic. Its decline began with its defeat by the Genoese at Meloria (1284) and continued as the Arno silted up – losing it vital access to the sea. In 1406 it was conquered by Florence, and the Medici rulers put their stamp on the city. They established its university, where the Pisan-born Galileo once taught.

Arriving in Pisa

Getting there
Pisa's main station is Pisa Centrale at piazza della Stazione. It's about a 20-minute walk to the piazza dei Miracoli. Buses from the airport stop opposite the station, and others come to nearby piazza Sant' Antonio. You can also get trains from the airport to Pisa Centrale. See Transport, page 74.

Getting around
Pisa is easy to explore on foot. Buses from the airport and railway station stop just beside the piazza dei Miracoli, so you can see the main sights even if you're just in the city for a couple of hours.

Tourist information
Tourist information office ① *piazza Vittorio Emanuele II, T050-42291, www.pisaturismo.it, Mon-Fri 0900-1900, Sat 0900-1330, daily 0930-1330*, and ① *Airport arrivals hall, T050-502518, aeroportoturismo@provincia.pisa.it, daily 0930-2100.*

Places in Pisa → For listings, see pages 73-74.

Piazza dei Miracoli
The 'Field of Miracles' is the name given to the grassy expanse that is the ecclesiastical heart of Pisa. At one time this was a rather marshy area, between two rivers: the (now invisible) Auser and the Arno. It was the site of an early Christian cathedral. It's here that you'll find the famous **Leaning Tower**, as well as the **Duomo**, the **Baptistery**, the **Camposanto** and two museums – the **Museo delle Sinopie** and the **Museo dell'Opera del Duomo**. These snowy marble buildings appear almost blindingly white in the sunshine. One edge of the piazza is lined with stalls selling an extraordinary range of tourist tat – look out for 'light-up' models of the Leaning Tower and 'leaning' mugs. You'll also see everyone taking their turn to do the 'comedy photo' – standing with the tower behind them, their hands poised as if they're holding it up.

Duomo

① Nov-Feb Mon-Sat 1000-1300, 1400-1700, Mar 1000-1800, Apr-Sep 1000-2000, Oct 1000-1900, Sun opens at 1300 all year.

Building of this magnificent cathedral began in 1063 (1064 in the contemporary Pisan calendar), when victory over the Saracens had brought Pisa enormous wealth. It was a statement to the world that this was a city to be reckoned with. Construction continued until the 13th century.

The cathedral represents the finest Pisan Romanesque style. The first architect, Buscheto, is buried in the wall on the left of the façade – an ornate construction built in the 12th century, which mixes Italian and Moorish influences. The three portals are topped with four tiers of colonnades and there are inlaid mosaics, stones and marble.

Inside, the cathedral is laid out in the shape of a Latin cross. It's a mix of styles, as a fire in the 16th century destroyed much of the original interior. There are Moorish black and white striped marble columns, a Byzantine-style gilded mosaic in the apse – which Cimabue completed in 1302, paintings by artists such as Beccafumi, and a 17th-century fresco in the dome. In the centre of the coffered ceiling you can see the Medici coat of arms. To the right-hand side of the altar is the mummified body of the city's patron saint, Ranieri, wearing a silver mask; to the left is the tomb of the Holy Roman Emperor Henry VII.

The most important work is the marble pulpit (1302-1310), which was sculpted by Giovanni Pisano. It is supported by the Virtues, Faith, Hope and Charity, and is covered with

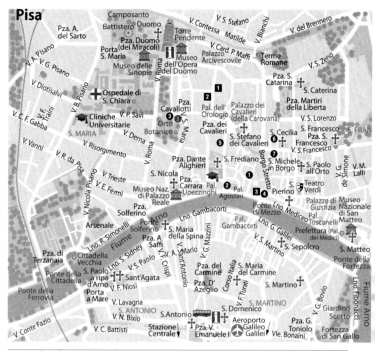

What to see in Northern Tuscany in...

...one day
See the main sights in Pisa (the **Leaning Tower**, the **Duomo** and the **Baptistery**), then catch a train to **Torre del Lago** on the coast, to visit the **Puccini Villa** or go on to **Viareggio,** famed for its *stile-Liberty* architecture. Or, spend a day exploring the lovely walled town of **Lucca** – essentials here are **San Martino Cathedral,** shopping on via **Fillungo,** a stop for some photos of the **piazza dell'Anfiteatro** and a walk (or cycle ride) around the ramparts.

...a weekend or more
Spend a day in Pisa, followed by a day in **Lucca.** Or – and perhaps more rewarding – spend one day in Lucca followed by a day's exploration of the **Garfagnana,** one of Tuscany's quietest corners. To take in **Pistoia** you'll need another day, especially if you want to drive to **Vinci** to see Leonardo's birthplace.

reliefs vividly depicting episodes from the New Testament. It is a masterpiece, the last of the great series of Pisano pulpits. After the fire it was dismantled and put into storage, and was eventually re-assembled in the early 20th century – though no-one can be completely certain that everything went back the way it was originally intended.

200 metres
200 yards

Where to stay ▭
Di Stefano **1**
Relais dell'Orologio **2**
Royal Victoria **3**

Restaurants ❼
Antica Trattoria Il Campano **1**
De'Coltelli **2**
Dolce Pisa **3**
La Bottega del Gelato **4**
Osteria dei Cavalieri **5**
Osteria del Tinti **6**
Osteria la Grotta **7**

Torre Pendente
ⓘ *Daily Nov-Feb 1000-1700, Mar 0900-1800, Apr to mid-Jun and Sep 0830-2030, mid-Jun to Aug 0830-2200, Oct 0900-1900. No children under 8. Tours only, advance booking essential in summer, recommended at other times. €18.*

Construction of this, the cathedral's bell tower, started in 1173. Due to the unstable, silty soil on which it was built and its shallow foundations, it began to lean before the third storey was completed – though it originally leaned the opposite way. Attempts were made to counteract this, and building then halted for 100 years. It continued in fits and starts until around 1350, with various architects, including Tommaso Pisano, attempting to correct the tilt – which now went the other way. The tower continued to tilt and by 1990 had reached a dangerous angle: experts estimated that if nothing were done it would collapse within 10 years. The tower was closed and a sophisticated programme of adjustment began. Rings of steel were placed around it, lead ingots were used as counterweights and soil was dug out

Pisa prices

Tickets are available at the ticket office at the Museo delle Sinopie, or the central ticket office by the tourist office near the tower. They are rather complicated. Admission to the Leaning Tower is €18 (pre-book online at www.opapisa.it), and entry is only by guided tours, every 30 minutes or so. No children under eight and no bags, only cameras. For the other attractions, the Duomo is free – but collect a coupon from the ticket office which covers two people, and €5 for each of the other sites if purchased individually. For any two attractions, the cost is €7 and for all four it is €9. Children under 10 go free, except for the Tower.

Bus 3 goes from the airport to Pisa station and then on past the Campo dei Miracoli. Get out at piazza Manin.

from underneath the northern side. These measures were successful and the tower now leans only as far as it did in 1838 – decidedly tipsy, but no longer dangerously drunk. It reopened in 2001.

The trip to the top involves climbing a narrow spiral staircase with – puff – 294 steps. The steps can seem slippery, as they slope so much in parts, and it can feel claustrophobic. However, it is a great way to truly appreciate the extent to which the tower leans.

Battistero

ⓘ *Daily Nov-Feb 1000-1700, Mar 0900-1800, Apr-Sep 0800-2000 (until 2200 in summer), Oct 0900-1900.*

The dazzling marble Baptistery was begun in 1152 and is the largest in Italy. Its shape resembles that of the Church of the Holy Sepulchre in Jerusalem. The first architect was Diotisalvi, but in the 13th century Nicola and Giovanni Pisano modified the building, which was eventually completed in the 14th century. It has a distinctive double dome, with an inner and outer cone, and fine acoustics. At busy times, on the hour and the half hour, attendants will shut the doors and demonstrate the echo. (Don't try it yourself, they'll tick you off.)

There is a large 13th-century font with inlaid marble panels, designed so that people could be baptised by total immersion. Most striking of all is Nicola Pisano's pulpit, which he completed in 1260. It was the first of the Pisano pulpits and was clearly influenced by Roman art.

Camposanto

ⓘ *Opening hours as for the Baptistery.*

Enclosed by long marble cloisters, the Camposanto or Holy Field is a walled cemetery, built on a site said to have been a burial area since Etruscan times. After the Third Crusade, at the end of the 12th century, the land was reputedly enriched with sacred soil brought from the Holy Land, and it was said that bodies buried here would decompose within 24 hours. Construction of the cloister itself began in 1278, and Roman sarcophagi, which had been re-used as tombs for wealthy Pisans (an early example of recycling), were brought here – you can see them as you walk around the cloisters.

At one time, the walls of the cloisters were covered with frescoes so stunning that they became an important sight on the Grand Tour. But the building was bombed in the Second World War, and the resultant fire melted the lead on the roof – which ran down the

The Pisano pulpits

There are four particularly famous pulpits in Tuscany, all carved by members of the Pisano family. Nicola Pisano (c1220/1225-1284) is considered the first great Tuscan sculptor. He came from Apulia, in southern Italy, and trained in the court workshops of Emperor Frederick II. He moved to Tuscany in the mid-13th century and around 1255 accepted a commission to create a pulpit for the Baptistery in Pisa. This, the first of the Pisano pulpits, represented a break with the past – it was no longer square, but a free-standing hexagon covered with relief panels. Look carefully at these and you can see how he drew on the traditions of ancient Rome but added life to his figures in characteristic Gothic style. In the nativity scene, you can see the Madonna leaning on her elbow and looking outward, looking rather like a Roman woman at a feast expecting to be fed grapes at any moment. Lions support the columns that hold the pulpit – one of them shows an interesting biological confusion: it has teats like a lioness, but the mane of a male lion.

After his success in Pisa, Nicola received a commission for another pulpit – this time for the Duomo in Siena. He worked on this with help from his son Giovanni, completing it in 1268. It's similar in design to the first but larger and even more magnificent. There are 300 figures on the panels and all have different faces. Although you can still see the classical influence, there is more drama and life here and the figures show emotions.

The third pulpit is in the Church of Sant'Andrea in Pistoia and was carved by Giovanni Pisano between 1298 and 1301. The panels here, notably the *Massacre of the Innocents*, are full of movement and energy; there is no central figure, but a tangle of characters all interacting. Here, well before Michelangelo, is an emotional depiction of suffering. Even the lionesses supporting the columns are more realistic – they don't have manes any more and one gently feeds her cubs.

The final pulpit is in Pisa's Duomo and is a masterpiece of the Italian Gothic. Carved by Giovanni in the early 14th century, it shows the extent to which he has been influenced by the Gothic style. Now the Madonna looks at her child rather than out to the viewer, and there is real desperation in the figures writhing in the *Massacre of the Innocents* panel. The series of pulpits provides a fascinating illustration of the evolution of sculpture in medieval Tuscany.

walls and destroyed most of the frescoes. You can see the survivors in the Frescoes Room: Buonamico Buffalmacco's lurid 14th-century cycles of *The Triumph of Death*, painted after the Black Death had swept through Tuscany, and *The Last Judgment*.

Take a look at the lamp that hangs under an arch in the cloisters. It is known as Galileo's Lamp and it is said that it once hung in the cathedral. Galileo, legend has it, observed it moving in the breeze, timed it with his pulse – and realized that it took the same number of beats to complete a swing no matter how far it moved. A pendulum, he concluded, could be used to measure time.

Museo delle Sinopie
① *Opening hours as for the Baptistery.*
This museum, on the opposite side of the piazza to the Camposanto, contains the preliminary sketches, known as *sinopie*, for the frescoes that lined the cloisters of the

Camposanto. These were revealed after the paintings were destroyed by the bombing and were later detached and displayed here. They got their name as they were made using paint pigmented with red earth from Sinop in Turkey.

Museo dell'Opera del Duomo
ⓘ *Opening hours as for the Baptistery.*
This museum, housed in an ex-convent near the Leaning Tower, contains statues and treasures from the main buildings in the piazza. There are carved tombstones, richly jewelled reliquaries, engravings and Roman and Etruscan objects. The most important work is a *Madonna and Child* (c1298) carved from ivory by Giovanni Pisano.

Piazza dei Cavalieri
A few streets away from the piazza dei Miracoli is this airy piazza, the historic seat of Pisan government. The most striking building, the *sgraffito*-covered **Palazzo della Carovana** (also known as the Palazzo dei Cavalieri), was remodelled by Giorgio Vasari in the 16th century. It housed an order of knights, the Cavalieri di Santo Stefano, established by the Medici ruler Cosimo I. They acted much like authorized pirates, frequently robbing ships of precious items. It is now a university, founded by Napoleon, specializing in maths and physics. Outside you can see a statue of Cosimo, his foot crushing a dolphin – symbolizing his victory over this maritime city and Medici dominion over the sea.

On the corner of the square, with an archway and clock, is the **Palazzo dell'Orologio**. The tower to the right of the clock is often known as the **Torre della Fame** (the Hunger Tower). This was where the Pisan Count Ugolino della Gherardesca was walled up, together with his sons, and left to starve, because the Pisans suspected him of treachery leading to their defeat at the Battle of Meloria. Dante describes the episode in his *Inferno* – according to him, the count ate the bodies of his children to stay alive.

From here you can walk down via Ulisse Dini and on to via Oberdan and Borgo Stretto: this is Pisa's slickest shopping street, lined with arcades and home to Salza, the city's historic *pasticceria*. Look out for the arresting frontage of the **Church of San Michele in Borgo**. Eventually you'll reach the Arno and the **ponte di Mezzo**. If you cross the river here the road becomes corso Italia, a busy – but less pricey – shopping street. Turn left and you can walk along the Arno to the **Museo Nazionale di San Matteo** ⓘ *Tue-Sat 0830-1900, Sun 0830-1330, €5/€2*), which houses a large collection of Tuscan art. Turn right, and you'll come to the **Museo Nazionale di Palazzo Reale** ⓘ *Mon-Fri 0900-1430, Sat 0900-1330, €5/€2.50*), a 16th-century palace that was the seat of the Medici court during the winter months. As well as portraits and tapestries, it houses a large collection of items associated with the annual **Gioco del Ponte** (see page 16). Not far from here is the **Orto Botanico**, Pisa's botanical garden – a lovely refuge in the heart of the city.

Pisa listings

For hotel and restaurant price codes and other relevant information, see pages 10-16.

⊖ Where to stay

Pisa *p67, map p68*

€€€€ Hotel Relais dell'Orologio, via della Faggiola 12/14, T050-830361, www.hotelrelaisorologio.com. This 14th-century fortified house has been turned into a 5-star hotel with plush rooms. Some feature frescoes, others coffered ceilings, and all are very comfortable – though very small. There's a courtyard garden and the hotel is very close to the Leaning Tower.

€€€ Bagni di Pisa, largo Shelley 18, San Giuliano Terme, T050-88501, www.bagnidipisa.com. The poet Shelley once stayed at this 18th-century villa, which evokes the grandeur of a more elegant age. Only 20 mins by train from Pisa, it makes a relaxing base for exploring the city and nearby coastline. They have a rooftop swimming pool and spa facilities – on arrival you're asked for your shoe and clothing size, so they can provide you with slippers and a robe. The buffet breakfast is excellent.

€€ Di Stefano, via Sant'Apollonia 35, T050-553559, www.hoteldistefano.it. The best rooms at this hotel are in the recently renovated 11th-century tower house. They have a contemporary Tuscan look, with some original features and fresh, clean bathrooms – some with jacuzzi baths. Facilities include flatscreen satellite televisions and a/c. Room 401, the top floor single room, has a cracking view of the Leaning Tower from its bathroom.

€€ Royal Victoria Hotel, Lungarno Pacinotti 12, T050-940111, www.royalvictoria.it. This riverside hotel seems to have changed little since it first opened in the early 19th century. The rooms have heavy, dark wood furniture and iron bedsteads, and some have frescoes. Bathrooms need a facelift. But the public areas are hung with fascinating photos, it has plenty of character and the rooms overlooking the Arno have fabulous views.

♉ Restaurants

Pisa *p67, map p68*

€€€ Antica Trattoria Il Campano, via Cavalca 19, T050-580585, www.ilcampano.com. Fri-Tue 1230-1500, 1900-2300, Thu 1900-2300. This trattoria in the market is in a medieval building with a vaulted ceiling and has some seats outside. Come for home-made pasta, with truffles or wild boar, and a good choice of wines.

€€ Osteria dei Cavalieri, via San Frediano 16, T050-580858, www.osteriacavalieri.pisa.it. Mon-Fri 1230-1400, 1945-2200, Sat 1945-2200. Fine Tuscan food, served with an imaginative twist, at this popular *osteria*. Dishes include courgette pudding, gnocchi with squash flowers and pistachio nuts, and Tuscan tripe. There are some 4-course set menus, including a vegetarian one for €26.

€€ Osteria la Grotta, via San Francesco 103, T050-578105, www.osterialagrotta.com. Mon-Sat 1200-1430, 1945-2230. Resembling a dark cave inside, with puppets of witches hanging on the walls, this *osteria* offers starters like toast with *lardo* and figs, filling soups and unusual pasta dishes like pistachio ravioli.

€€ Osteria del Tinti, vicolo del Tinti 26, T050-580240, www.osteriadeltinti.it. Thu-Tue 1900-2400, Sun also 1230-1500. Good local food, tucked away down a side street. Their pasta dishes include *testaroli* with pecorino and olive oil, and they also do gnocchi with monkfish and lemon sauce.

Cafés and bars

De' Coltelli, Lungarno Pacinotti 23, T050-541611. Daily 1130-0100 (shorter hrs in winter). Delicious ices on the Arno.

Dolce Pisa, via Santa Maria 83, T050-563181. Sat-Thu 0730-2000. Not far from the Orto

Botanico, this is a good place to stop for lovely pastries and espresso.

La Bottega del Gelato, piazza Garibaldi 11, T050-575467. Daily, summer 1100-0100, closes earlier and on Wed in winter. Many locals rate this as the best *gelateria*. Prepare to queue.

❀ Festivals

Pisa *p67, map p68*
Jun
Celebrations for Pisa's patron saint: on 16 Jun the façades of all the palaces along the Arno are illuminated with candles; on 17 Jun there is a boat race on the river, and on the last Sun in the month rival *contrade* take part in the Gioco del Ponte.

⦿ Shopping

Pisa *p67, map p68*
Food and drink
Il Vecchio Forno, via Domenico Cavalca, corner of Vicolo del Tidi, piazza del Campano, T050-580488. Daily 0900-1400, 1600-2000. All sorts of lovely handmade sweets and cakes, such as Pisanini buns and cantucci.

Market
Piazza Vettovaglie. Daily 0730-1330. Pisa's food market, where you can buy picnic supplies and bottles of olive oil to take home. It sells fruit, vegetables, cheese and more.

⊖ Transport

Pisa *p67, map p68*
Frequent trains go from Pisa to **Florence** (1 hr 20 mins), **Lucca** (20 mins) and **Viareggio** (18 mins). Trains also go to **Pistoia** (1 hr 16 mins), sometimes requiring a change at Lucca. There are slow irregular trains from Lucca to **Barga** (36 mins) but Barga station is outside the town and you will need to take a taxi.

❶ Directory

Pisa *p67, map p68*
ATMs Corso Italia, piazza Garibaldi and via Oberdan. **Hospitals** Ospedale di Santa Chiara, via Roma 67, T050-992111/996111 (no A&E). **Cisanello**, via Paradisa 2, 3 km from the city centre, T050-992300 (First Aid); T050-992 111, www.ao-pisa.toscana.it.
Pharmacies Farmacia Comunale, 5, via Niccolini 6a, near piazza dei Miracoli (24 hrs), and Salvioni, via Oberdan 3.

Viareggio and the coast

From both Pisa and Lucca, it is easy to take a train to spend a day at the coast. Viareggio is the liveliest and most famous of Tuscany's seaside resorts, the golden sand almost invisible under the endless rows of sun loungers. Famous today for its carnival, it was a fishing village until the 16th century, when it became the Republic of Lucca's only coastal base. By the late 19th century Viareggio was growing as a seaside resort, reaching its heyday in the 1920s and 1930s. As you walk around you can see the *stile-Liberty* buildings erected in that era – though some of them now look neglected.

Places in Viareggio and on the coast → *For listings, see page 76.*

Just 6 km south of Viareggio – you can take a bus from piazza d'Azeglio – is **Torre del Lago**. This was, for many years, the home of Giacomo Puccini. The great composer lived in an elegant villa by Lake Massaciuccoli, where he had peace and quiet and could indulge his love of shooting: he claimed his rifle was his "second favourite instrument". **Museo Villa Puccini** ① *T0584-341445, www.giacomopuccini.it, Tue-Sun, Apr-May 1000-1230, 1500-1800, Jun-Oct 1000-1230, 1500-1830, Dec-Mar 1000-1230, 1430-1730, €7, guided tours last around 40 mins*, is filled with Puccini's original furnishings, musical instruments, rifles and memorabilia. It was here that he composed most of his operas, including *La Bohème*, *Tosca* and *Madama Butterfly*. In 1921 he moved to Viareggio, where he lived until his death in 1924. He is buried in the chapel at Torre del Lago.

This part of the coast is much less developed than Viareggio, with fragrant pine forests and rich birdlife. The lake is part of the **Parco Regionale di Migliarino**, **San Rossore**, **Massaciuccoli** (www.parks.it) and there are a number of visitor centres (T0584-975 5677) where you can arrange birdwatching trips, guided walks and boat trips.

Viareggio and the coast listings

For hotel and restaurant price codes and other relevant information, see pages 10-16.

🛏 Where to stay

Viareggio *p75*

€€€€ Principe di Piemonte, piazza Giacomo Puccini 1, T0584-4011, www.principedipiemonte.com. Lots of *stile Liberty* and Murano glass at this plush hotel. Each floor is furnished in a different style, with the fifth floor being the most modern. There's an outdoor rooftop pool and a good-quality restaurant.

€€€ Hotel Plaza e de Russie, piazza d'Azeglio 1, T0584-44449, www.plaza ederussie.com. This hotel, in a late 19th-century building not far from the harbour, has comfortable bedrooms, marble bathrooms and a rooftop terrace restaurant with great views.

Camping

There are 2 campsites near Viareggio: **Viareggio,** via dei Comparini 1, T0584-391012, www.campingviareggio.it, open mid-Mar to end Sep; and **Camping Paradiso,** via dei Tigli, T0584-392005, www.campingparadisodiviareggio.com.

🍴 Restaurants

Viareggio *p75*

€€€€ Bagno Ristorante la Rondine, Terrazza della Repubblica 33, T0584-53130. Daily 1230-1430, Thu-Sat 2000-2230. At the far end of the seafront, at the Citadelle di Carnevale end, this quality restaurant specializes in locally caught fish. Specialities include tagliatelle with *bottarga*, and mixed fried fish.

€€€ Cabreo, via Firenze 14, T0584-54643. Lunch and dinner. Closed Mon. In a quiet side street, with its own little courtyard, this restaurant offers a variety of fish dishes – such as gnocchi with lobster sauce. You can also find pasta dishes like tagliatelle with beef.

€€€ La Darsena, via Virgilio 150, T0584-392785, www.trattorialadarsena. it. Mon-Sat 1200-1430, 1945-2230. This fish restaurant by the harbour area offers dishes such as seafood risotto and spaghetti with clams. Their mixed grill is a speciality. Desserts include home-made cakes.

🎭 Entertainment

Viareggio and the coast *p75*
Clubs

The coastline around Viareggio is noted for its nightlife – head for Forte dei Marmi, Viareggio and Marina di Pietrasanta. The gay scene is lively on the coast at Torre del Lago.

Nightspots include: **BK2 Balena 2000,** Lungomare Margherita, via Modena, Viareggio T0584-44045, www.b2k.it; **La Canniccia Club,** via Unita d'Italia, Marina di Pietrasanta, T0584-23225, Sat from 2300; **La Capannina di Franceschi,** Forte dei Marmi, T0584-80169, www.lacapanninadi franceschi.it; **Mama Mia,** Torre del Lago, T393 22 393 22, www.mamamia.tv, Apr-Sep daily 2400-0400, Oct-Mar Fri-Sun 2100-0200; **Seven Apples,** viale Roma 108, Marina di Pietrasanta, T0584-20458, www.sevenapples.it, Fri-Sun. Many clubs close in winter and **Twiga,** viale Roma 2, Marina di Pietrasanta, T0584-21518, www.twigabeachclub.com, Fri-Sat.

Lucca

Lucca, the birthplace of Puccini, is a delightful place to visit – the historical centre is immaculately preserved within its city walls. Despite its small size, Lucca was once a significant force in Tuscany. It was the capital of the Lombard Duchy of Tuscia, which was more important in its time than Florence, and continued to be a powerful centre under the Frankish rulers. In fact the Duchy of Lucca (as it became) remained essentially independent until Napoleon's era, and the city today radiates a confidence born of centuries of power. Lucca is still extremely prosperous and has a large British community.

Arriving in Lucca

Getting there
The railway station is just outside the city walls at piazza Ricasoli. You can get buses or taxis from here into the centre. There are frequent trains from Pisa (20 minutes) and slow irregular trains from Barga (36 minutes).

Getting around
Most of the historic centre of Lucca is pedestrianized – the locals buzz around on bicycles. You can get buses or taxis from the railway station that will take you within the city walls. To explore the Garfagnana you really need a car. The railway station is just outside the city walls at piazza Ricasoli. You can get buses or taxis from here into the centre.

Tourist information
Tourist information office ① *piazzale Verdi, T0583-583150, www.luccaturismo.it/ www.luccaitinera.it, daily Easter-31 Oct 0900-1900, 1 Nov-Easter 0900-1700.* The office at piazza Santa Maria 35 was closed at the time of writing.

Places in Lucca → *For listings, see pages 82-83.*

Duomo di San Martino
① *Piazza San Martino, www.museocattedralelucca.it. Daily, summer Mon-Sat 930-1745, Sun 0930-1045, 1200-1800; winter Mon-Fri 0930-1645, Sat 0930-1745, Sun 0930-1045, 1200-1700 free. Sacristy: mid-Mar to early Nov Mon-Fri 0930-1745, Sat 0930-1845, Sun 0900-1045, 1130-1800, early Nov to mid-Mar Mon-Fri 0930-1645; Sat 0930-1845; Sun 0930-1045, 1200-1700, €3, €7 joint ticket with Museo della Cattedrale and San Giovanni.*
Lucca's magnificent cathedral was founded way back in the sixth century, though the present building is largely medieval. The façade is eye-catching as it's not symmetrical – it was built on to an earlier bell tower, dating from 1060, which sits at the right-hand corner of the façade. It makes a striking sight – a fine example of Pisan Romanesque style, with three

tiers of ornate marble columns sitting above a portico. This is filled with carvings created by Lombard sculptors in the 13th century, including a *Deposition from the Cross* and an *Adoration of the Magi* by Nicola Pisano – essentially the first of the great Tuscan sculptors.

The Holy Face Once inside the cathedral you can see its most important treasure, a wooden crucifix known as the *Volto Santo* (Holy Face). Made of cedar of Lebanon, the face is said to be a true portrait of Christ, which was carved by Nicodemus – and finished by an angel – in the Holy Land. Nicodemus was a witness to the Crucifixion. In fact the work is said to be a 13th-century copy of an earlier carving. The Holy Face is thought to have miraculous powers – King William Rufus of England literally swore by it: "*Per sanctum vultum de Luca*" was his customary oath. It was said to have journeyed to Lucca all by itself, by boat and then on a cart pulled by oxen, and its presence in Lucca made the cathedral an important pilgrimage site during the Middle Ages. This, of course, brought considerable wealth to the town. The Holy Face is kept in an ornate shrine within the cathedral, and every September there are celebrations in its honour: there is a procession through the city and the figure of Christ is dressed in an embroidered tunic and gold crown.

The Sacristy In the Sacristy you can see a beautiful early Renaissance carving, the **tomb of Ilaria del Carretto** (1407). The second wife of a local nobleman, Paolo Guinigi, Ilaria died in childbirth aged just 24, and this work was created in her memory by Jacopo della Quercia.

Round the ramparts

Built in the 16th century to defend the city against hostile neighbours, Lucca's walls are almost perfectly preserved and have not only limited the town's size but have also helped to preserve its ancient buildings and Roman street patterns. The effect is even said to have rubbed off on its people, as the *Lucchese* (those born and bred inside the walls) are said to be particularly conservative.

The town has an ancient history and has built a succession of defensive walls – each enclosure being wider and more elaborate than the last. The earliest walls, built by the Romans, have largely disappeared today, but remnants can still be seen inside the Church of Santa Maria della Rosa. A larger circle of walls was built during medieval times, and these were extended and strengthened during the 16th century, so as to withstand bombardment by the most up-to-date missiles – cannon balls. However, the work took so long that by the time the new walls were completed they were no longer needed.

Today the walls still seem to act as a barrier – only this time to the modern world rather than invaders. They're broad and lined with trees, providing a convenient cycling, walking and jogging track (a 4-km circuit), used by locals and tourists alike. You can easily get on to the walls from any of the bastions and the tourist office has details of bike hire.

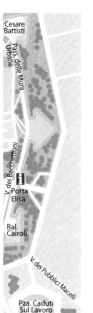

200 metres
200 yards

Where to stay 🛏
Albergo San Martino **1**
Alla Corte degli Angeli **2**
Ilaria **4**
La Boheme **5**
Palazzo Alexander **6**
Palazzo Tucci **7**

Restaurants 🍴
Antico Caffè delle Mura **10**
Antica Locanda dell'Angelo **1**
Buca di Sant' Antonio **2**
Caffè Di Simo **3**
Gelateria De'Coltelli **11**
Gelateria Veneta **4**
Il Mecenate a Lucca **12**
Locanda di Bacco **5**
Rewine **13**
Ristorante Giglio **6**
Taddeucci **7**
Trattoria da Leo **8**
Vineria i Santi **9**

She lies, sculpted in marble, on top of the tomb – a delicate figure who looks as if she's sleeping, with a dog at her feet as a symbol of fidelity. The Sacristy also contains a *Madonna and Child Enthroned* by Ghirlandaio.

Museo della Cattedrale
ⓘ *Piazza San Martino, T0583-490530, www. museocattedralelucca.it. Mar-Nov daily 1000-1800, Nov-Mar Mon-Fri 1000-1400, Sat 1000-1800, Sun 1000-1700, €4 or joint ticket as above.*

Across the square from the cathedral, this museum contains the cathedral's treasures displayed in a medieval building. Among them are the richly jewelled items with which the *Volto Santo* is dressed each year: his shoes, his crown and a silver girdle. There are also illuminated texts and a Limoges enamel box depicting the martyrdom of St Thomas à Becket.

Chiesa di Santi Giovanni e Reparata
ⓘ *Piazza San Martino, www.museo cattedralelucca.it. Mar-Nov daily 1000-1800, Nov-Mar Sat-Sun 1000-1700, €4 or joint ticket as above.*

Lucca's villas

Lucca is a wealthy city, partly due to silk (it was noted for the quality of its underwear) and olive oil, and it's surrounded by grand villas that were built as summer homes by wealthy merchants between the 15th and 19th centuries. You can easily spend a day touring these villas, some of which are within a short distance of the city. The gardens alone are well worth seeing.

One of those closest to Lucca is the **Villa Reale** (Marlia, T0583-30108, www.parcovillareale.it, March to end November, gardens only 1000-1300, 1400-1800, sometimes guided tours only), which once belonged to Napoleon's sister. The violinist Paganini, her court composer, played here, and John Singer Sargent painted the grounds. Further on is **Villa Mansi** (Segromigno, T0583-920234, Tuesday-Sunday summer 1000-13000, 1500-1800, shorter hours in winter, €8), a former silk merchant's house, and the baroque **Villa Torrigiani** (Camigliano, T0583-928041, daily March-November, 1000-1300, 1500-1830, grounds only €7, grounds and villa €10), built in the early 16th century by the Buonvisi family. It was later bought by the Marquis Nicola Santini, who was Lucca's ambassador at the court of the Sun King, Louis XIV of France. Santini had the garden transformed, with a parterre and ornamental ponds. He also added grottoes and *giochi d'acqua* – surprise water features, which would soak unsuspecting guests.

On the other side of the cathedral square, this church was Lucca's original cathedral. It was built in the fourth century, but has been altered many times since then. Excavations have revealed a number of ancient structures beneath the church, including a Roman mosaic floor, a Roman bath and an early Christian baptistery.

San Michele in Foro
① *Piazza San Michele. Daily summer 0800-1200, 1500-1800, winter 0900-1200, 1500-1700, free.*
San Michele rather outshines Lucca's Duomo, so lavish is its façade and so lively its location. The piazza on which it sits is the historical heart of the city – the former Roman forum. A church stood here in the eighth century, though this building dates from the 11th century on. The medieval façade is an extraordinary confection of twisted columns and rich carvings. Look carefully (not easy, as it's several storeys high) and you'll see it's decorated with allegorical scenes, wild birds and animals and topped with a winged statue of St Michael the Archangel.

Inside it's surprisingly restrained. The large cross by the altar was made by local artists around 1200 (pre-Giotto), and there's a terracotta by Andrea della Robbia by the door. The most important work is Filippino Lippi's painting of *Four Saints*.

Note how small the windows are: this church is Romanesque in style, with rounded arches, in which most of the weight has to be borne by the walls. The later Gothic style employed pointed arches, which are more stable than rounded ones and can bear weight themselves. This allowed Gothic churches to have larger windows, making them lighter inside.

Museo Casa Natale di Giacomo Puccini
① *Corte San Lorenzo 9, off via di Poggio, T0583-584028, www.puccinimuseum.org, Apr-Oct 1000-1800; Nov-Mar 1100-1700, closed Tue, €7.*

Lucca was the birthplace of one of Italy's most famous composers, Giacomo Puccini (1858-1924) and the house where he was born has been turned into a museum. It's small but stuffed with sheet music, letters and other memorabilia. In pride of place is the grand piano on which he composed his last opera, *Turandot*; he died before he could complete it. A statue sits in the square nearby.

Museo Nazionale di Palazzo Mansi
ⓘ *Via Galli Tassi 43, T0583-55570, www.luccamuseinazionali.it, Tue-Sat 0830-1930, €4, free under 18 and over 65. Join ticket with Museo Nazionale Villa Guinigi €6.50.*
This former aristocratic home, dating back to the 16th and 17th centuries, is now a museum and art gallery. It's worth visiting just to see the utter grandeur of the rooms, decorated with frescoes and hung with rich tapestries. Most striking is the Baroque honeymoon suite, a confection of gold, carved woods and silk. There are paintings by Tintoretto, Bronzino and a portrait by Pontormo of Alessandro de' Medici, who was murdered in 1537.

Piazza Anfiteatro
It's hard to stop taking pictures of this elegant piazza, which was once a Roman amphitheatre, built in the second century. Although the original buildings have been replaced by private houses, the distinctive curved shape remains, giving the place an air of drama. Today it's a great spot to chill out, as it's full of shops, bars and cafés, with tables spilling out on to the piazza. It's tucked away off the north end of **via Fillungo**, one of Lucca's main shopping streets. Some of the shops are rather like museums in themselves, especially **Carli**, a jeweller that dates back to 1655. You'll also find **Caffè di Simo** (closed at the time of writing), which has original *stile-Liberty* décor and once boasted Puccini as one of its customers.

Basilica di San Frediano
ⓘ *Piazza San Frediano, T0583-493627, daily summer 0900-1200, 1500-1700, winter 0900-1200, 1500-1800, free.*
The façade of this church, which dates back to the 12th century, is covered with a stunning gilded mosaic in Byzantine style, depicting Christ with his Apostles. The interior is impressive too, with fragments of frescoes adorning the walls. Look out for the enormous baptismal font, to the right of the entrance, richly decorated with carvings depicting stories from the Old and New Testaments – including Moses crossing the Red Sea. In a side chapel is the uncorrupted body of St Zita, a 13th-century saint, which is brought out once a year for people to touch. The basilica was built on the site of a sixth-century church founded by St Fredian, an Irish monk who rose to become Bishop of Lucca.

Palazzo Pfanner
ⓘ *Via degli Asili, T0583-954029, www.palazzopfanner.it, Apr-Oct daily 1000-1800, early Nov Thu-Mon 1100-1600, €4.50 garden, €6 garden and palace.*
A local family of silk merchants built this 17th-century palace, which was bought in the 19th century by an Austrian brewer, Felix Pfanner. It has a grand staircase that sweeps up to some equally grand rooms (only part of the palace is open to the public). Loveliest of all are the gardens, filled with roses, citrus trees and statues – if you think it looks like a film set you'd be right: the gardens featured in *The Portrait of a Lady* (1996), which starred Nicole Kidman. You get a great view of the gardens from the city ramparts.

Lucca listings

For hotel and restaurant price codes and other relevant information, see pages 10-16.

🛏 Where to stay

Lucca *p77, map p78*

€€€ Palazzo Tucci, via Cesare Battisti 13, T0583-464279, www.palazzotucci.com. You'll feel as if you're staying in your own private palace at this gorgeous residence on the 1st floor of an 18th-century palace. Just a discreet brass doorbell proclaims its presence; inside are 3 large rooms and 3 suites, all with original features such as flamboyant frescoes. Bathrooms are large, there is elegant period furniture, and one room has a small terrace. The ballroom makes it a great venue for a small wedding.

€€ Albergo San Martino, via della Dogana 9, T0583-469181, www.albergosanmartino.it. There are 10 rooms at this friendly 3-star hotel. They're small and clean, decorated in pastel colours with private bathrooms, all with showers. In summer you can breakfast outside on the little street-side terrace, and it's very close to the Duomo.

€€ Alla Corte degli Angeli, via degli Angeli 23, T0583-469204, www.alla cortedegliangeli.com. Spread over 3 floors, this B&B has 10 small but clean rooms – and plenty of character. Each room is different, many have frescoes and all have private bathrooms.

€€ Hotel Ilaria, via del Fosso 26, T0583-47615, www.hotelilaria.com. Situated close to the city walls, this 4-star hotel makes a comfortable base for exploring the city and its surroundings (it has private parking). There's a pleasant lobby with comfy sofas, free Wi-Fi and complimentary hot drinks and snacks. Rooms are clean and light, with flatscreen TVs and tea and coffee making facilities. There's a terrace with sun beds placed under the trees, and free bicycle hire.

€€ La Boheme, via del Moro 2, T0583-462404, www.boheme.it. There are just 5 rooms at this friendly, central B&B. One room has a 4-poster bed. Bathrooms are small but clean, and there is a/c. The breakfast room is light and fresh – though you can breakfast in your room if you prefer.

€€ Palazzo Alexander, via Santa Giustina 48, T0583-583571, www.palazzo-alexander.it. There's a touch of 18th-century gilded grandeur to the rooms and suites in this historic residence, with its period furniture, swagged curtains, shiny wood floors and gold bedcovers. Bathrooms can be small but are modern and clean, with marble fittings and hairdryers. Breakfast is an elegant affair: a buffet of dainty pastries, fresh fruit and yoghurts. The staff are consistently friendly and helpful – always a bonus.

🍴 Restaurants

Lucca *p77, map p78*

€€€ Antica Locanda dell'Angelo, via Pescheria 21, T0583-467711, www.locanda dellangelo.it. Tue-Sat 1200-1430, 1930-2200, Sun 1200-1430. This family-run restaurant is tucked away on a side street near piazza Napoleone. A courtyard terrace at the back means you can dine outside. There are 2 set menus – 'creative' and 'Tuscan', and you can also order à la carte – ravioli with sea bass and celery cream perhaps, or swordfish with tomato and mint.

€€€ Buca di Sant'Antonio, via della Cervia 3, T0583-55881, www.ristorantilucca.it. Tue-Sat 1230-1500, 1930-2200, Sun 1230-1500. Dating back to 1782, this is Lucca's most famous restaurant – Puccini used to eat here and it still attracts the great, the good, locals and visitors. The interior is full of character, with copper pans hanging from the ceiling, and the food – traditional Lucchese – is consistently good.

€€€ Locanda di Bacco, via San Giorgio 36, T0583-493 1363, www.locandadibacco.it. Wed-Mon 1200-1530, 1900-2230. Intimate restaurant with dark wood interiors, offering typical food of the region. Dishes include pork with cannellini beans and rosemary, and tortelli lucchese – meat-filled pasta with ragù. There's a 5-course tasting menu too. A few doors down, at number 26, is its cheaper sister restaurant, **Osteria Via San Giorgio**.

€€€ Vineria i Santi, via dell'Anfiteatro 29a, T0583-496124, www.vineriaisanti.it. Thu-Tue 1230-1500, 1930-2300. This stylish *vineria*, its walls lined with wine bottles, is behind the Anfiteatro. It offers contemporary versions of traditional dishes, such as fusilli pasta with Chianina beef ragù or stuffed rabbit with potatoes and spinach. Desserts might include a walnut and fig tart. Around 400 Tuscan wines to choose from too.

€€ Il Mecenate a Lucca, via del Fosso 94, T0583-512167, www.ristorantemecenate.it. Look for traditional Tuscan dishes such as chickpea flour crepes with ricotta, pumpkin ravioli, Cinta Senese (pork from Siena) and roasted salt cod.

€€ Ristorante Giglio, piazza del Giglio 2, T0583-494058, www.ristorantegiglio.com. Thu-Mon 1200-1430, 1930-2200, Wed 1930-2200. You'll find queues at this restaurant, which offers pasta and dishes such as bean soup with spelt, and rabbit with olives and corn mash. There are tables outside; eat inside and you'll be surrounded by flamboyant frescoes – the building was a palace in the 18th century.

€ Trattoria da Leo, via Tegrimi 1, T0583-492236, www.trattoriadaleo.it. Mon-Sat 1200-1430, 1930-2230. This established trattoria attracts both locals and tourists, who come for the lively atmosphere and hearty dishes such as pasta with meat sauce and fried chicken with vegetables. Plenty of seats outside – but no credit cards accepted.

Cafés and bars

Antico Caffè delle Mura, piazzale Vittorio Emanuele 2, T0583-464552, www.caffedellemuralucca.it. This is a restaurant and coffee bar on top of the city wall.

Caffè di Simo, via Fillungo 58, T0583-496234. Daily 0930-0030. This has long been the best known of all Lucca's cafés, worth seeing for its turn-of-the-century interior of dark wood with marble and glass fittings. Locals come in to play chess and chat. It is closed at the time of writing.

Gelateria De'Coltelli, via S Paolino 10 (near piazza S Michele), T0583-050667. Home-made ice cream.

Gelateria Veneta, via Vittorio Veneto 74, T0583-467037, www.gelateriaveneta.net. Daily 1000-0100 in summer, closed Nov-Feb. Lucca's most famous *gelateria*.

Rewine, via Calderia 6, T0583-48427. Tue-Sat 0800-2200, Mon evening and 3rd Sun in month. This contemporary bar does a good range of aperitifs, ideal for an early evening drink.

Taddeucci, piazza San Michele 34, T0583-494933, www.taddeucci.com. This café proudly proclaims that Prince Charles is a former customer. It's famed for its *buccellato* (aniseed and sultana bread) and also does unusual tarts, such as a sweet vegetable tart with pine nuts and spices.

❶ Directory

Lucca *p77, map p78*
Banks ATM at piazza San Michele.
Medical services Hospital: Campo di Marte, via dell'Ospedale, T0583-9701. Pharmacy: Farmacia Alliance, piazza Curtatone 9 (24 hrs), Farmacia Massagli, piazza San Michele 36, and G. Giannini, piazza San Frediano 1.

The Garfagnana and the marble mountains

The Garfagnana is a glorious area. It's the mountain valley of the Serchio River – a land of thick chestnut forests, little towns, country churches and sleepy hamlets, where few tourists come. There are lots of possibilities for walking and wildlife watching, and if you've got a car the winding roads (watch the hairpin bends) lead you through some stunning scenery. You can explore some of it in a day from Lucca, but to really appreciate its quiet charm it's better to take a couple of days.

Places in the Garfagnana and the marble mountains → *For listings, see pages 85-86.*

The SS12 from Lucca shadows the river to **Diecimo** (the name comes from the fact that it was 10 Roman miles from Lucca), near which you can see one of the oldest churches in the valley, which has been populated since Paleolithic times. From here you can continue to **Celle dei Puccini** (where the composer's family once lived) and the **Museo del Castagno** ⓘ *Colognora, T0583-358159, www.museodelcastagno.it, Sun and holidays 1500-1730 and on reservation T0583-358004; closed in winter.* Chestnuts have long been immensely important to the local economy: they are ground into flour and used in both sweet and savoury dishes.

Continue north and you reach **Borgo a Mozzano**, where the 14th-century Devil's Bridge spans the river. The name comes from a legend that says the devil built the bridge in return for the soul of the first to cross it: the villagers sent a dog and 'outwitted' him (though who says dogs don't have souls?).

The road soon branches, going east to **Bagni di Lucca**, a fashionable spa town in the 19th century, or heading north towards **Barga**. This ancient hill town is a great place to stop for an hour or so. Its cathedral (free) dates back to the ninth century and stands on the town's highest point, offering glorious views across to the Apuan Alps. Inside is a magnificent marble pulpit, which stands on columns supported by two lions and a crouching man. Outside, look above the portal to the left of the entrance to see a famous carving of a feast. Barga has extremely strong links with Scotland, and you'll hear many Scottish accents there. Local people migrated to Glasgow in the 19th century, some selling plaster statues of saints, others seeking work in the shipyards. They settled, and were followed by friends and family, many of whom started businesses making ice cream or frying fish and chips. Famous Glasgow Italians include the actress Daniella Nardini, whose family originally came from Barga.

From Barga you could cross the valley and head west to visit the **Grotta del Vento** ⓘ *www.grottadelvento.com, daily Apr-1 Nov, 26 Dec-6 Jan tours hourly from 1000-1800, €9; rest of year open Sun and holidays*, or Cave of the Wind. These caves are filled with stalactites, stalagmites, secret passages and underground lakes. Various tours are available, lasting from one to three hours. Otherwise, you can drive on to **Castelnuovo di Garfagnana**, the main town, where you can pick up plenty of information and maps on walking in the region.

From here you can follow the roads northeast, high into the mountains, to **San Pellegrino in Alpe**, where there's a museum devoted to rural life. Alternatively, take the **Cipollaio road** that leads southwest, crossing the mountains and down to the coast. This was an ancient route used by pilgrims and has a wild, lonely feel. You'll pass **Isola Santa**, a medieval village that was deserted when a hydroelectric dam was created there in 1949. After this the scenery changes, the mountains look bare and forbidding and you enter marble country. The Romans started quarrying for marble here and it continues today – marble from **Carrara** is famous throughout the world. You will pass an abandoned marble quarry, drive through a tunnel and come down to **Seravezza** – where Michelangelo was sent by the Medici Pope Leo X to find the best marble he could for the church of San Lorenzo in Florence. He didn't like the area, considering it wild and rough. The air is filled with marble dust.

You can drive from here to the coast and **Forte dei Marmi**, or turn off to **Pietrasanta**, a chic little walled city that has long been a magnet for sculptors and has a thriving artistic community. Contemporary sculptures are displayed in the lively piazza del Duomo and there's a bronze of a warrior by Fernando Botero in piazza Matteotti. The Duomo was built in the 14th century and has a stunning rose window. Take a look at the pulpit – the staircase that leads to it was made by Andrea Baratta in the 17th century from a single block of marble. Pietrasanta has plenty of studios and workshops open to the public – it's a great place to pick up original artworks. Check out the **Associazone Artigianart** website for addresses: www.artigianart.org.

The Garfagnana and the marble mountains listings

For hotel and restaurant price codes and other relevant information, see pages 10-16.

⊖ Where to stay

The Garfagnana and the marble mountains *p84*
€€€ Palazzo Guiscardo, via Provinciale 16, Pietrasanta, T0584-792914, www.palazzo guiscardo.it. This *stile-Liberty* building has been transformed into a small hotel, with just 9 rooms. Bathrooms are fitted with local marble and furnishings are plush, with period pieces, plump cushions and rich colours.
€ Fortezza di Monte Alfonso, piazzetta Ariosto 1, Loc. Montalfonso 55032 Castelnuovo di Garfagnana, T0583-62616, www.luccaturismo.it, www.montalfonso.it. This fortress is gradually being converted into a welcome centre for the Garfagnana, and has 7 hostel-type rooms in converted outbuildings. These are very clean, have bunk beds and sleep 2-8 people. There's also a restaurant where you can have breakfast.

Self-catering
Ai Frati, località ai Frati 19/A, 55036 Pieve Fosciana, T0583-65378, www.agriturismo aifrati.com. This is a 14th-century monastery, converted into an *agriturismo*. The 5 small apartments (€650 per week) have been created out of monks' cells. It's surrounded by grounds and has a pool. Most atmospheric are the cloisters, with their crumbling walls. There is also a bedroom that can be rented by the night (€85).
I Cedri, località Alla Villa 4, 55020 Albiano-Barga, T0583-765270, www.agriturismo icedri.it. La Filanda is a former silk factory, on the **I Cedri** estate about 10 mins' drive from Barga. There are well-tended grounds and an outdoor pool, and the views of

distant Barga are glorious. The estate produces wine and olive oil. 3 apartments are available for weekly rentals.

❷ Restaurants

The Garfagnana and the marble mountains *p84*

€€€ Enoteca Marcucci, via Garibaldi 40, Pietrasanta, T0584-791962, www.enoteca marcucci.it. Tue-Sun evenings. Lively family-run *enoteca*, with communal wooden tables, candlelight and a cellar stocked with around 2000 wines. The food is good as well – they are noted for their steaks.

€€ L'Osteria di Riccardo Negri, piazza Angelo 13/14, Barga, T0583-724547. 1200-1500, 1900-2200. Sunflowers on the terrace make this *osteria* in the centre of Barga bright and welcoming. The menu changes daily, but you might find nettle ravioli, ravioli filled with spinach and ricotta, or grilled beef. For dessert, try a home-made cake.

€ Al Laghetto, località Pontaccio, Turrite Cava, Gallicano, T0583-75798. Wed-Mon 1200-1500, 1900-2300. They're noted for their meats at this large restaurant set among the trees. Try a mixed grill, or delicious potatoes cooked very simply in ashes in the wood-fired oven. They also do excellent flatbreads with different fillings.

€ Da Sci, via Nazario Sauro 2, Pietrasanta, T340-272 6685. Home-made pasta and traditional, good value Tuscan food at this family-run trattoria in Pietrasanta. It's very popular with locals.

€ Osteria Vecchio Mulino, via Vittorio Emanuele 12, Castelnuovo Garfagnana, T0583-62192, www.ilvecchiomulino.com. Tue-Sun 0730-2030. You could easily pass by this excellent *osteria*, perched on a corner. Inside are original wood fittings, wooden tables and Andrea Bertucci, the owner, encouraging you to try his home-cured meats, local cheeses and bread. Desserts are freshly made – perhaps a chestnut torte or ricotta cake.

€ Ristorante Molino della Volpe, località Molino della Volpe, Gello, Pescaglia, T0583-359045, off Diecimo–Pescaglia road, by sign to Celle dei Puccini. Mon-Tue, Thu-Sun 1900-0100, also Mon and Sat-Sun 1200-1430. This is a charming countryside restaurant in a converted mill. The seasonal menu uses typical products of the Serchio Valley, such as mushrooms, pumpkins and chestnuts. If you ask in advance, they can prepare some old recipes using chestnut flour.

€ Rita e Rinaldo, Focchia 9, 55060 Pescaglia, T0583-357728, off Pascoso-Diecimo road. Thu-Tue. Just a handwritten wooden sign directs you to this little country restaurant, run for over 40 years by Rita and her husband Rinaldo. Tables outside give views over the valley, and dishes might include tortelli pasta with ragù, rabbit with olives and *sformato di verdure* – vegetable pie.

Cafés and bars

Caffè Capretz, piazza Salvo Salvi 1, Barga, T0583-723001. Tue-Sun 0745-approx 2200. Historic café that once played host to Garibaldi. There is outdoor seating – the terrace at the back has the best views.

Pistoia and around

Pistoia is one of Tuscany's best-kept secrets, a small city with a rich history and a fine medieval square. It sits surrounded by fertile countryside dotted with plant nurseries and mountain villages, but because of its strategic position (squeezed between Lucca and Florence), life was not always so tranquil. The city folk once had a reputation for violence: in the 13th-century the Guelphs here divided into rival factions: the Blacks and the Whites.

Pistoia was a Roman settlement, and some think that the city's name comes from the *pistores*, the Latin name for the many bakers who worked here. Another theory gives the name Etruscan roots, from *pist oros* – 'mountain gate' – as the city lies at the foot of the Appenines. Visitors are often disappointed not to find lots of shops selling pistols, as some say a *pistole* was once a type of dagger, and its name was later given to a locally made firearm.

The city was put on the map in the 12th century when a relic of St James was brought here and it became a stop on the via Francigena. Its striking medieval piazza del Duomo is much larger than you'd expect, with buildings representing ecclesiastical and secular power taking equal precedence.

Places in Pistoia → *For listings, see pages 91-92.*

Duomo di San Zeno

ⓘ *Piazza del Duomo. Daily 0830-1230, 1530-1900, free, €2 to get close to the silver altarpiece.*

This cathedral dates back to AD 923, though it was remodelled in Pisan Romanesque style from the 12th century, as you can see from the zebra-striped marble and tiered arcades. Before you go in, take a look at the statue on the top right of the façade, wearing the red cloak – it is St James wrapped in a pilgrim's mantle. In the archway above the entrance are colourful tiles by Andrea della Robbia.

Inside the cathedral, to the right of the entrance, is the tomb of Cino da Pistoia – a poet and a friend of Dante. Then you come to the most outstanding work in the cathedral, the **Altarpiece of Saint James**, tucked into a side chapel. This silver altar was made to hold the holy relic and is decorated with over 600 figures, with scenes from the Old and New Testaments, the life of Saint James and the apostles. It was started in 1287 and not completed until the 15th century. Over 40 artists and craftsmen were involved in its creation, including a young Brunelleschi. You have to pay to see it up close, but it's worth it, as only then can you appreciate the details, the progression in artistic styles and the gleaming gemstones inlaid into the silver.

Also in the cathedral is a 13th-century gilded wooden crucifix, of the school of Cimabue. The colours are bright: gold, turquoise and lapis lazuli. In the chapel to the left of the altar is a painting, the *Madonna di Piazza*, which is said to be the only signed work by Andrea del Verrocchio (c1435-1488), an artist at the Medici court who had Leonardo da Vinci as a pupil. It is thought that he started the work, but it was completed by Lorenzo di Credi.

Around piazza del Duomo → *For listings, see pages 91-92.*

Beside the Duomo is the **Bell Tower** (tours at weekends 1100-1200 and 1600-1700, book at the tourist office). It was built as a watchtower. Look at the crenellations on top: the swallowtail shape is a sign that this was a Ghibelline town: Guelph walls had square crenellations. However, given how often loyalties changed, architectural details were not always accurate indicators.

On the other side of the Duomo is the wall of the former **Palazzo dei Vescovi** (Bishop's Palace). It houses the tourist information office and the Museo di San Zeno (temporarily closed for restoration) which contains the reliquary of Saint James. Downstairs are the remains of the Roman town.

Opposite the Duomo is the 14th-century **Baptistery** ⓘ *Tue-Sun 1000-1300, 1500-1800, free*, a black and white striped marble octagon designed by Andrea Pisano. In the Baptistery tickets can be purchased to visit the tower and see the silver altarpiece.

Via di Stracceria is an atmospheric street that was the heart of medieval commercial life in Pistoia. You can still see the rustic-style porticoes and wooden shutters on the shops. It leads on to **piazza della Sala**, the heart of daily life in the city, where the market is held. **Vicolo della Torre** is another interesting city street, connecting the Bishop's Palace to piazza della Sala.

Chiesa di San Giovanni Fuorcivitas

ⓘ *Via Cavour. Daily 800-1100, 1730-1830 though often closed.*

This church, once outside the city walls (*fuorcivitas*), is notable for the green and white marble stripes that cover its north wall. Inside is a large pulpit, carved by a pupil of Nicola

Pisano, while the basin holding the holy water is by Giovanni Pisano. To the left of the door is a *Visitation* by Luca della Robbia. One of his earliest works, it is in white glazed terracotta and depicts Elizabeth, pregnant with John the Baptist, kneeling at the feet of Mary.

Chiesa di Sant'Andrea
ⓘ *Via Sant'Andrea, T0573-21912. Daily 0930-1300, 1500-1900.*
The foundations of this church date back to the eighth century, though the present building is largely 12th century. Above the door is a Romanesque relief of the *Journey of the Magi*, while inside is one of Pistoia's greatest treasures, a marble pulpit carved by Giovanni Pisano, the third in the series of the great Pisano pulpits.

Near here is the **Ospedale del Ceppo** (piazza Giovanni/via del Ceppo). Founded in the 13th century, this is still a functioning hospital. It's named after the offertory box (*ceppo*) in which alms were collected for the sick. The building is notable for its fine portico, which was decorated with a frieze in the 16th century. It depicts all the functions a hospital would then have fulfilled.

Around Pistoia → *For listings, see pages 91-92.*

Montecatini Terme and around
You can get a train from Pistoia to this historic spa town. Development really began in the 18th century and Montecatini soon became a fashionable health resort. At the beginning of the 20th century, extravagant buildings were constructed around the springs at Parco delle Terme. The most impressive is **Tettuccio**, where you can buy a day ticket to taste the waters. There are four waters on offer here, flowing from different taps. Each has its own name and characteristics: Leopoldina is very strong and laxative, so be warned ("It will work in 20 minutes," declares an attendant. "We have 600 toilets.") Regina is considered full of calcium and good for the liver; Tettuccio is salty, considered good for lowering cholesterol. These three fountains are turned off in the afternoon, but Rinefresco, the lightest water, is available all day. (For information on the spas, T0572-772244, www.montecatiniturismo.it and T0572-7781, www.termemontecatini.it.)

Allow time to take the **funicular railway** ⓘ *daily Apr-Oct, €7*, uphill to the original medieval settlement of **Montecatini Alto**. It bumps upward through olive groves and thick trees, and you get superb views at the top. The square has a number of restaurants. (The funicular stops for lunch between 1300 and 1430. Check the times: if you get stuck at the top a taxi would cost around €20.)

If you have a car visit some of the hill towns near Montecatini. There're not full of 'sights', but the atmosphere and views are very pleasant. West of Montecatini at **Colle di Buggiano**, for instance, you can see San Lorenzo Church, which contains a 14th-century wooden crucifix, while at **Buggiano Castello** there is 11th-century San Nicolao Church, which contains an *Annunciation* (1442) attributed to Bicci di Lorenzo. There's a great picnic spot just here – a bench near the church with stunning views. **Montevettolini** (southeast of Montecatini, near Monsummano Terme) is another pretty village, with a 13th-century town hall and a café/*enoteca* on the main piazza. The Medicis built a mansion here. There's a good, family-run restaurant at **Monsummano Alto**: La Foresteria ⓘ *T0572-520097, www.ristorantelaforesteria.it.*

Vinci

Surrounded by silvery olive groves, a few kilometres south of Pistoia, Vinci is famous as the birthplace of the ultimate Renaissance man, Leonardo da Vinci. There's a wooden model of his *Vetruvian Man* on the town's panoramic terrace. The sights are low key but the countryside is deliciously tranquil, with plenty of walking trails to follow.

Pop into the **Chiesa di Santa Croce** in the village, as this is where Leonardo was baptised. You can walk from Vinci to Anchiano, 2 km away, to visit the **Casa Natale di Leonardo** ① *daily Mar-Oct 0930-1900, Nov-Feb closes 1800, free*. This three-roomed house is where Leonardo was born in 1452. Inside, there's little to see, just an exhibition on the great man and some lovely views.

Museo Leonardiano

① *Palazzina Uzielli, T0571-933251, www.museoleonardiano.it, Mar-Oct daily 0930-1900, rest of year closes at 1800, ticket office closes 1 hr before the museum shuts, €7, 6-14s €5.*

The museum is essentially split between two sites (the other is the Castello dei Conti Guidi nearby) and focuses on Leonardo's extraordinary inventions, with scale models of the machines he invented – ranging from an automatic weaving loom to a flying machine.

Pistoia and around listings

For hotel and restaurant price codes and other relevant information, see pages 10-16.

🛏 Where to stay

Pistoia and around *p87*

€€ Tenuta di Pieve a Celle, via Pieve a Celle 158, T0573-913087, www.tenuta dipieveacelle.it. On the outskirts of Pistoia is this excellent *agriturismo* in an elegant villa set in its own grounds. The immaculate rooms all have private bathrooms, and there's a comfortable lounge with fresh flowers and lots of books and magazines. The owners use produce from their organic garden for breakfast (and dinner, which they cook on request). There's a swimming pool, vineyard and free bike hire.

€ Canto della Porta Vecchia, via Curtatone e Montanara 2, T0573-27692, www.dormireintoscana.it. Press the brass bell, go up 3 flights of stairs and you're in this lovely B&B run by Anna Bresci. There are just 4 rooms, only one with its own bathroom, but they're lovely and clean with original frescoes, a tiny terrace and stunning views from the lounge. Friendly and central.

€ Le Pòggiola, via Treggiaia 13, T0573-51071, www.lepoggiola.com. Just 10 mins from the centre of Pistoia is this lovely farmhouse. They have double rooms (minimum 3 nights' stay) – some with shared bathrooms – as well as 1 self-catering apartment sleeping 4. Lisa, the charming owner, can give cookery lessons if you wish and organize tours of the farm, with oil and wine tastings. There's a swimming pool too. Lisa also has a separate self-catering residence, Il Vallone, in Monsummano Terme (www.tenutailvallone.it).

Self-catering

ArteMura Residence, via Pietro Bozzi 6/8, T0573-366698, www.artemuraresidence.com. There are 20 beautifully furnished apartments in this former palace. All are different – the

most unusual is the Tower Room – and they vary in size, sleeping 2-6. The residence also has a lovely secluded garden.

Casa Carbonaia, San Lucia, via di S. Lucia 11, near Anchiano, T0571-993252, T(+34) 348-791 1215, www.casacarbonaia.com. Just a few mins' drive from Leonardo's birthplace is this country farmstead, converted into 7 apartments. They make a great choice for families. There's a pool and plenty of walking and cycling routes nearby. Minimum stay 3 nights.

Nido del Merlo, via Montalese 67, T0573-479602, www.nidodelmerlo.it. The Bindini Family don't speak English, but they're so friendly and welcoming it doesn't matter. They have 2 self-catering apartments sleeping up to 6 and 4 simply furnished B&B rooms (**€**). It's not a quiet retreat but a slice of Italian life. There's a small pool, you can borrow bikes and bus 19 will take you into Pistoia.

Self-catering

La Porta di Mignana, via Mignana 67, Vitolini, T0571-584726, www.casavacanze laporta.it. This rustic Tuscan building a short drive from Vinci has been converted into 5 self-catering apartments sleeping 2-4. It's a popular choice with families. There is also a swimming pool.

🍴 Restaurants

Pistoia and around *p87*

€€ CacioDivino, via del Lastrone 13, T0573-194 1058, www.cacio-divino.it. Mon-Sat 1000-1500, 1800-2300. Light blue walls and cheery napkins give this place a youthful feel. There's a blackboard menu and an excellent selection of tasting plates. The *crostone* make a good light lunch.

€€ La BotteGaia, via del Lastrone 17, T0573-365602, www.labottegaia.it. Tue-Sat 1030-1500, 1830-0100, Sun 1830-0100. A lovely *osteria* where you can just drop in.

Come for tagliatelle with beef, or beans and rosemary, or *panzanella* with greens.
€ **Da Ale**, via San Anastasio 4, T0573-24108. Daily 1930-2430, closed Mon in winter. This pizzeria, set in a former church, is quite small and gets very busy. There are paper placemats and no frills, but the pizzas are delicious.

Cafés and bars
Sadly Pistoia's historic **Caffè Vailiani**, which once served coffee and pastries to figures like Verdi, Rossini and Puccini, has closed down. In its absence try the following:
Bar Michi, piazza del duomo, T0573-976381, www.michiwinebar.it.
Gelateria Monterosa, via Dalmazia 397, T0573-402075. Take viale Europa exit off ring road. Mon-Tue and Thu-Sat 1530-2300, Sun 1030-late. Arrigo Merlini makes his ice creams on the premises and locals like them so much they drive here to sample them.
Pasticceria Armando, via Curtatone e Montara, 38, T0573-23128.

Eastern Tuscany

The eastern corner of Tuscany has plenty to offer the visitor who's keen to discover the region's hidden corners. Traversed by the busy A1 *autostrada* that links Rome to the north, it's a combination of busy industrial districts and outlet shops with quiet hill towns and gloriously tranquil forests. Arezzo, about an hour by train from Florence, is the main centre and the springboard for a trail of works by Piero della Francesca, the acclaimed early Renaissance painter who was born in nearby Sansepolcro and spent most of his life in this part of Tuscany.

South of Arezzo is Cortona, a deliciously picturesque town with pre-Etruscan origins and steep, winding streets, which attracts legions of tourists in summer. It's set on a hill that rises steeply from the reclaimed marshes of the Valdichiana, the flat agricultural plain on which Chianina beef cattle are raised.

To the north of Arezzo are quiet hill towns such as Poppi and Bibbiena, and the extensive woodlands of the Casentino, a protected area that offers excellent possibilities for walking and cycling.

What to do in Eastern Tuscany in...

...one day

If you've got a car, do a whistle-stop version of the Piero della Francesca trail. Starting in **Arezzo**, make your first call **San Francesco Church** to see his *Legend of the True Cross* frescoes. Stroll round the piazza Grande, then on to the **Duomo** to see Piero's *Mary Magdalene*. After lunch, drive to **Monterchi** to see the famous *Madonna del Parto*. Your final stop is **Sansepolcro**, Piero's birthplace.

...a weekend or more

You have time to enjoy both the main centres. Spend a day in **Arezzo**, visiting sights such as the 12th-century **Pieve Santa Maria** and the **Ivan Bruschi museum**, as well as Piero della Francesca's frescoes. Next day, take a train to picturesque **Cortona**, where you can take a stroll round the shops, visit the **Etruscan Museum** (MAEC) and the **Museo Diocesano**, which is the home of Fra Angelico's *Annunciation*.

Arezzo → *For listings, see pages 102-107.*

Arezzo is a prosperous working city with Etruscan origins. The lower part is busy and modern, the upper part well tended and medieval. Once a month it fills to bursting with thousands of Italians, attracted by the large antiques market that spills out of the main square into the surrounding streets. This is fun if you want to browse among the stalls and experience local life, but best avoided if you're on a whistle-stop artistic pilgrimage, as it's frustratingly hard to move around the city.

Arriving in Arezzo

Getting there and around Arezzo is small enough to explore on foot and is closed to tourist traffic anyway. There's a car park near the train station by piazza della Repubblica though spaces are hard to find; buses also stop nearby. There are regular buses between Arezzo and Cortona-Camucia. See Transport, page 107.

Tourist information Tourist information office ① *piazza della Repubblica 28, T0575-377678, www.apt.arezzo.it, daily 0900-1300, 1500-1900 (shorter hours out of peak season).*

Basilica di San Francesco

① *Piazza San Francesco, T0575-352727/299071, www.apt.arezzo.it. Nov-Mar Mon-Sat 0900-1730, Sun 1300-1730, Apr-Oct Mon-Fri 0900-1830, Sat 0900-1730, Sun 1300-1830. Entry to frescoes on the hour and half hour, €6 plus €2 booking fee (booking essential in high season, booking office next to church), free 5-18/EU citizens/over 65, but booking fee applies; church free.* This huge Franciscan church is most people's first stop in Arezzo, as it's the home of some of Piero della Francesca's most famous works. But the church would be worthy of a visit even without their presence: the walls are covered with fascinating fragments of frescoes, which were painted as a sort of 'bible of the poor' to make the Christian story accessible to the illiterate. The oldest of them date from the 1380s. There's also a huge 13th-century wooden crucifix over the altar, the work of an Umbrian artist. It's noteworthy as an early example of a depiction of Christ as a suffering man, rather than simply a divine being.

Just beside the ticket barrier, near the altar steps, is an unusual 15th-century tomb on the wall. It is credited to Michele da Firenze, who had worked as an assistant in Lorenzo Ghiberti's workshop while he was creating the north doors of the Baptistery in Florence.

The tomb is made in coccio pesto, a kind of stucco made from crushed terracotta, which gives it a distinctive salmon colour. It was used by the Romans to make pavements, as it could withstand high temperatures, and da Firenze revived the technique. You can see other examples in the **Santissima Annunziata** in via Garibaldi and on a lunette above a doorway outside the cathedral.

The frescoes Behind the altar are Piero della Francesca's frescoes illustrating the *Legend of the True Cross*, which were painted some time between 1452 and 1466. This

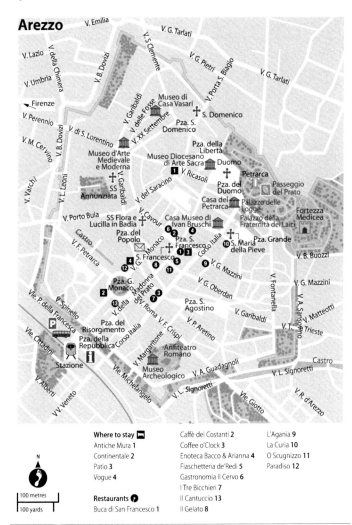

100 metres
100 yards

was a time when the Christian West felt threatened: the Ottoman Turks had taken Constantinople, causing the collapse of the Byzantine Empire, and the frescoes reflect some of those contemporary fears.

Piero della Francesca (c1412/1420-1492) was born in Borgo San Sepolcro (now Sansepolcro) and spent much of his life in the environs of that little town. He served some time as an apprentice painter in Florence, where he worked with Domenico Veneziano. He was an academic artist, particularly interested in perspective and geometry – on both of which he wrote respected treatises. He was invited to carry out the work in San Francesco after the original artist, Bicci di Lorenzo, died. (You can see di Lorenzo's work on the ceiling.)

The frescoes were badly damaged by damp and it took 15 years – and a great deal of money – to restore them. Work began in 1991. To get a proper look at them you need to go beyond the altar steps, and for that you have to buy a ticket. The panels don't follow a narrative order but are arranged to be most aesthetically appealing: structure, symmetry and geometry were important to Piero. So you have to jump from one to another to follow the story, which was taken from a 13th-century text by Jacopo da Varazze: *Legenda Aurea*.

The tale starts at the top with Adam's death, and a seed planted on his grave growing into the tree that eventually made the Cross. It moves down to show the Queen of Sheba kneeling before a beam that she recognizes as part of this holy tree – and which she realizes will form the Cross of the Crucifixion. Solomon orders the wooden beam to be buried. One of the most famous panels is on the back wall, bottom right, in which Emperor Constantine has a dream in which an angel tells him that he will defeat his enemies by giving up his weapons and fighting under the sign of the Cross. Constantine sleeps under a tent, which appears to be softly illuminated (the effect is rather more obvious if you stand back, near the altar). It's one of the first night scenes by an Italian painter.

Panels on the other side wall include one in which a man is dropped down a well to force him to say where the Cross is buried; and one in which, out of three possibilities, the True Cross is discovered when it resurrects a dead man. The last one, at the top of this wall, shows the Cross returning to Jerusalem.

Piazza Grande

The town's medieval piazza is an unusual trapezoidal shape, with a distinct slope. On one side is a 16th-century **arched loggia** designed by local man Giorgio Vasari: it's essentially the first shopping mall, with swish apartments above and shops underneath. It was reserved for the wealthy, and a sign remains reminding members of the lower orders that they'd be subjected to the local equivalent of the stocks if they were found under the hallowed arches. Now some smart restaurants mingle with antiques shops, which, along with those on via di Seteria, look like antiques themselves.

Pieve di Santa Maria

ⓘ *Corso Italia, 7, T0575-22629, Oct-Apr 0800-1200, 1500-1800, May-Sep 0800-1300, 1500-1900, free.*

You enter this church, which backs on to the piazza Grande, from corso Italia. Built in the 12th century, it was originally the town's cathedral. Steps by the altar lead to the choir, where there's a painted cross dating from 1262 and a polyptych by Pietro Lorenzetti, painted in 1320. The façade has three tiers of columns, which get closer together and smaller. Some, in an early example of recycling, are Roman. Sculptures above the door show scenes from each month of the year – May is represented by soldiers going to war: apparently it was the favoured season for fighting.

Duomo

ⓘ *Piazza del Duomo, T0575-23991, daily 0630-1230, 1500-1830, free.*

Although the cathedral was started in 1277, work carried on for centuries (the bell tower wasn't completed until 1936). It's noted for its **stained-glass windows** (1516-1525) by Guillaume de Marcillat, a French Dominican friar, and they're distinctive, with architectural backgrounds, bright colours and flesh tones in the people's faces. In one, depicting Christ driving the money-lenders out of the temple, there's a man in a red hat who seems to be running straight at you, no matter where you stand. (It's on the right hand side as you look at the altar.) Near the tomb of Pope Gregory is a small fresco of *Mary Magdalene* (c1459) by Piero della Francesca, in which he demonstrates his knowledge of perspective. She's holding an opaque apothecary's jar – a local tradition always depicts her as a bearer of myrrh. The church also contains the ornate **tomb of San Donato**, Arezzo's patron saint. A neighbouring column, topped with an oil lamp, is said to be the one on which he was beheaded.

La Casa Museo di Ivan Bruschi

ⓘ *Corso Italia 14, T0575-354126, www.fondazionebruschi.it. Tue-Sun 1000-1300, 1400-1800 (summer 1000-1800), €5 6-18s/over 65s €3.*

The home of a famous antiquarian (1920-1996 – who started the local antiques fair) contains his enormous collection of antiques and oddities from around the world. It's spread over three floors and includes everything from Etruscan urns to African statues. There are displays of his stamps (arranged in patterns stuck into albums), household items, glassware, books and gold coins. Be sure to go up to the terrace on the very top floor: it allows you to see the detail on the columns of the Pieve opposite.

Chiesa di San Domenico

ⓘ *Piazza San Domenico, daily 0800-1900, free.*

This church was mostly constructed in the 13th century. You can see fragments of later frescoes on the walls. It's most famous for a **crucifix by Cimabue**, Giotto's teacher. The work, dating from 1260-1265, at first looks Byzantine, but then you see that Cimabue has departed from convention by depicting Christ as a suffering man: you can see the tensed muscles in the body, and the blood coming from the wounds realistically coagulating. A few drops have even fallen on to the golden frame.

Museo Archeologico

ⓘ *Via Margaritone 10, T0575-20882, daily 0830-1930 (though may be closed in low season), 6, free under 18/EU citizens over 65.*

On the edge of town, this museum is next to the **Roman amphitheatre**, which is thought to date from the second century AD. Some estimates suggest it could have held 13,000 people. You can view it for free. The museum itself contains important finds, including a vase attributed to the Greek painter Euphronius and Etruscan and Roman artefacts including bronzes and jewellery. Don't miss the coral-coloured ceramic vases, which were produced in workshops in Arezzo during Roman times and were widely exported.

Fortezza Medicea and Prato

ⓘ *Viale Bruno Buozzi, daily, free.*

Not far from the Duomo, a public park leads to this fortress (under restoration at the time of writing). It was built in the 16th century by the Florentines, who destroyed houses, churches and lanes in the process. It's generally quiet and gives good views of the town and the distant mountain. The park makes a great picnic spot. There's a kiosk café/bar, which opens intermittently.

Casa Vasari
ⓘ *Via XX Settembre 55, T0575-409040, Mon and Wed-Sat 0830-1900, Sun 0830-1300, €4, under 18s/EU citizens over 65s free.*
This was the home of Giorgio Vasari (1511-1574), who was born in Arezzo and became an influential artist and architect. He was court painter to Cosimo de' Medici and has often been called the first art historian: he wrote *Lives of the Most Excellent Painters, Sculptors and Architects*, in which he traces the development of art from the time of Cimabue. He designed this house and decorated it himself with lavish frescoes.

Monterchi → For listings, see pages 102-107.

Museo della Madonna del Parto
ⓘ *Via Reglia 1, Monterchi, T0575-70713, Apr-Oct 0900-1300, 1400-1900, Nov-Mar 0900-1300, 1400-1700, closed on Tue, €5.50, under 14s/pregnant women free.*
A rather unremarkable former school in the small village of Monterchi is the home of one of the most unusual paintings in Western art: Piero della Francesca's *Madonna del Parto* (1450-1468). It depicts Mary while pregnant, with angels parting the curtains around her as if she's on a stage. You almost expect them to cry 'Ta-ra!' The church used to disapprove of such a human depiction of the Madonna, but they've come round to the idea now. Some think it was a homage to the artist's mother, who was born in Monterchi.

The fresco used to be in a church in the town, but was detached and moved to another chapel in the 18th century. It was eventually restored in 1992 at a cost of over €100,000 and is now displayed alone in a glass case. Other rooms in the museum are given over to detailed descriptions of the restoration. The painting has become a point of pilgrimage and women hoping to have a child will often come here to pray before it.

Sansepolcro → For listings, see pages 102-107.

Museo Civico
ⓘ *Via Niccolò Aggiunti 65, T0575-732218, mid-Jun to mid-Sep daily 0930-1330, 1430-1900, mid-Sep to mid-Jun 0930-1300, 1430-1800, €8, 10-18s €3, under 10s free.*
The town was the birthplace of Piero della Francesca, and the former town hall is now a museum containing some celebrated examples of his work. There's the *Madonna della Misericordia* (1445-1461), an early polyptych, richly gilded and displaying his distinctive geometric forms. There's also his fresco of the *Resurrection of Christ* (1458-1474), which depicts Christ standing in a landscape with one raised foot resting on the edge of his tomb; soldiers sleep beneath him, one of whom, dressed in brown, is said to resemble the artist. Aldous Huxley once declared this painting "the best picture in the world", and his description saved it (and Sansepolcro) from destruction by the Allies in the Second World War, because the officer who was to order the bombardment had read Huxley's essay. Other works in the museum include a large ceramic *Nativity* by della Robbia: look closely and you'll see that it was made as a 'jigsaw'.

Aboca Museum

ⓘ *Via Niccolò Aggiunti 75, T0575-733589. Oct-Mar Tue-Sun 1000-1300, 1430-1800, Apr-Sep 1000-1300, 1500-1900, €8, 10-14s €4.*

A former palace that's been turned into a fragrant museum of herbalism – a pleasant change if you've had your fill of high culture. There are carefully illustrated old herb books, huge majolica storage jars, masses of dried herbs, an old apothecary's shop and a 'poison cell', where toxic remedies were tucked behind an iron grille. Pick up one of the informative brochures before you look round, as the labelling's in Italian.

Duomo

ⓘ *Via Matteotti, daily early-1200, 1530-1830, free.*

Sansepolcro's cathedral had its origins in the 11th century and is in Romanesque-Gothic style. The most striking feature of its façade is a fine rose window – when you stand inside you can see the panes of alabaster with which it is glazed.

The cathedral contains a gilded 14th-century polyptych of the *Resurrection*, attributed to Niccolò di Segna: the central figure of Christ stands in a pose so similar to Piero della Francesca's in the Museo Civico that many feel Piero must have studied this painting. There's also a 10th-century woodcarving of *Christ on the Cross*.

Cortona → *For listings, see pages 102-107.*

There are enough museums and works of art in Cortona to occupy you for a couple of days at least – Fra Angelico and Luca Signorelli are the stars. It's also a good base for exploring the villages of the Valdichiana and nearby Lago Trasimeno. However, it's much more commercialized than Arezzo. It's been besieged by visitors ever since American author Frances Mayes set up home here in the 1990s and wrote about her experiences in *Under the Tuscan Sun*, which was later made into a film. Late spring and summer are particularly busy. Not all the locals approve of visitors on this modern literary trail. They did, as one said, "have Fra Angelico long before Frances Mayes".

Arriving in Cortona

Getting there and around Cortona is small enough to explore on foot, however many of the streets are extremely steep and would be difficult for anyone with mobility problems to negotiate. The city centre is closed to tourist traffic. There are car parks outside the walls of Cortona but spaces are very hard to find in high season. Cortona's railway station, Camucia, is about 6 km out of the city centre. Buses stop at piazza Garibaldi. There are regular trains and buses to Arezzo and Camucia. See Transport, page 107.

Tourist information Tourist information office ⓘ *via Nazionale 42, T0575-630352, May-Sep Mon-Sat 0900-1300, 1500-1900, Sun 0900-1300, winter closes at 1800 Mon-Sat and closed Sun.*

Museo dell'Accademia Etrusca e della citta' di Cortona (MAEC)

ⓘ *Palazzo Casali, piazza Signorelli 9, T0575-637235, www.cortonamaec.org, Apr-Oct daily 1000-1900, Nov-Mar Tue-Sun 1000-1700, €10. To arrange visits to the tombs, ask at the museum or T0575-630415/612565.*

You can't miss the prize exhibit here: an **Etruscan bronze oil lamp** from the fourth century BC, hanging from the ceiling of its own little temple on the first floor. It was probably

Fra Angelico

One of the most celebrated of the early Renaissance artists, Fra Angelico was born Guido di Pietro near Fiesole in around 1387. He became a Dominican friar in 1407, together with his brother, taking the name Giovanni. A talented artist, influenced by Giotto, his works were intended to stimulate prayer and meditation. He prayed before starting work and his paintings are notable for their tenderness and glorious colours. It was said that he was so devout that tears would pour down his face as he painted.

He initially trained as an illuminator. John Ruskin said he was "not an artist ... [but] an inspired saint" and Vasari called him "humble and modest". When he had completed the Annunciation, now in Cortona's Museo Diocesano, he said: "When I saw this work, I nearly fainted dead from shock and love of it. I could not have done it alone. I sighed and wept." He spent four years in Cortona, and worked all over Tuscany as well as in Rome. Known in Italy as *Beato Angelico* (the 'blessed' Angelico), he died in 1455 and is buried in Rome. His epitaph contains the words: "The deeds that count on Earth are not those that count in Heaven. I, Giovanni, am the flower of Tuscany." He was beatified in 1982.

designed for an important sanctuary and looks much like a chandelier. It's covered with ornate carvings of goddesses and priapic satyrs, with a gorgon at the centre. The rest of the floor is filled with cases displaying serried ranks of Etruscan bronzes – all the more mysterious because they're not labelled. There's a swaddled baby, horses, a delicately worked swan and mice nibbling at ears of corn. At the end are paintings by Luca Signorelli and his nephew. For great views of the countryside, go on to the terrace, which links two parts of the upper floor.

Other exhibits cover everything from Egyptian artefacts – including a wooden funerary boat – to Tuscan paintings. From the Roman era there's a mosaic pavement and a *glirarium* – a shelved urn used for breeding and fattening dormice, a favourite Roman dish. On the lower floor are finds from Melone del Sodo, the Etruscan tomb just outside the town. They include an exquisite gold panther and delicate jewellery, and a scale model of the tomb gives some idea of its sophistication. MAEC's website shows two routes you can follow – one inside and one outside the city – to see this and the other main archaeological sites.

Museo Diocesano
ⓘ *Piazza del Duomo, T0575-62830. Apr-Oct daily 1000-1900, Nov-Mar Tue-Sun 1000-1700, €5, 6-12s €3.*
Made of two former churches, this museum contains some stunning works of art. Turn right when you enter to see Fra Angelico's superbly delicate, gilded *Annunciation* (c1430), painted when he lived in Cortona for a few years. On the wall to the right is another of the master's works, a triptych of the *Madonna with Child and Four Saints*. Other artists represented in the museum include Sassetta, Pietro Lorenzetti and Luca Signorelli. On the ceiling of the **Lower Oratory** downstairs are frescoes of Old Testament scenes designed by Vasari. Twentieth-century works by the Futurist artist Gino Severini, born in Cortona, line the stairs.

Chiesa di San Domenico
ⓘ *By piazza Garibaldi, daily but sometimes closed, free.*
The sun is fading one of this Gothic church's most precious items: a lunette above the door frescoed by Fra Angelico (c1433-1434). Inside is a 16th-century altarpiece by Luca Signorelli.

Chiesa di Santa Margherita
ⓘ *Piazzale Santa Margherita, T0575-603116, winter daily 0830-1200, 1500-1800, summer 0730-1200, 1500-1900, free.*
There's been a church on this site since 1297, built in honour of St Margaret of Cortona. The present church was built in the 19th century. It's got an eye-catching blue ceiling and a rose window made by Giovanni Pisano. In pride of place is the intact body of St Margaret, set in a glass coffin. Should you wish to, you can press a switch to light it up.

You can walk to the church from Cortona by following the **viale Santa Margherita**. It joins an ancient track, possibly used by medieval pilgrims, along which are the *Stations of the Cross* decorated with mosaics by the artist Gino Severini.

Around Cortona → *For listings, see pages 102-107.*

Convento delle Celle
ⓘ *3.5 km east of Cortona, T0575-603362, www.lecelle.it, 0800-1930, free.*
Set in a peaceful hollow beside a gushing stream, this monastery was built by St Francis in 1211 and enlarged over the centuries. Built in creamy stone on the craggy slopes of Monte Sant'Egidio, it's immensely evocative. You can visit the original chapel and St Francis' tiny cell, with its wooden bed and wooden pillow. He used to stop here regularly on his travels and visited just four months before he died in 1226.

Frantoio Landi
ⓘ *Località Cegliolo 71, Mezzavia, a 15-min drive from Cortona, T0575-612814, www.frantoiolandi.it.*
If you fancy some olive oil, take a trip out to Frantoio Landi, a family-run olive mill. Olives are collected and pressed between granite stones in the traditional way – they'll give you a tour of the factory – and in season (November/December) you can watch the pressing. The family's own oil is for sale.

Eastern Tuscany listings

For hotel and restaurant price codes and other relevant information, see pages 10-16.

🛏 Where to stay

Arezzo *p94, map p95*

€€€ Hotel Vogue, via Guido Monaco 54, T0575-24361, www.voguehotel.it. Not only does this hotel have contemporary rooms, they boast original bathroom features: Leoparda has a freestanding bath behind the bed, and Michelangelo has a double 'massage' shower. Each room has TVs, high-quality fittings and a careful blend of historic features and up-to-the minute style.

€€ Hotel Continentale, piazza Guido Monaco 7, T0575-20251, www.hotel continentale.com. Clean and comfortable, with a central location, pleasant staff and a lovely terrace with views of the cathedral. The hotel is gradually being refurbished; at the time of writing rooms on the 1st floor are fresh and bright, with newly tiled bathrooms. At the very top are 3 new suites (**€€€€**), decorated in French style with contemporary bathrooms.

€€ Hotel Patio, via Cavour 23, T0575-401962, www.hotelpatio.it. This stylish small hotel has quirky Bruce Chatwin-themed suites, featuring different aspects of the great writer's travels. Baalbek, for example is pink and yellow, with a mosquito net over the bed, while Wu-Ti is red and cream. 2 new rooms are contemporary and uncluttered in shades of beige, and feature chromotherapy baths. There's Wi-Fi access in all rooms.

€ Antiche Mura, Piaggia di Murello 35, T0575-20410, www.antichemura.info. 6 light, stylish rooms at this friendly new B&B, set on the 1st floor of a 13th-century building. On the top floor is a room with a panoramic view of the city. Breakfast is included in the price, but taken in the nearby Bar Il Duomo – space is reserved for you in their pretty courtyard.

Self-catering

Agriturismo Montemiliano, località Borgacciano, near Monterchi, T0575-709030, www.montemiliano.it. You'll get glorious views of historic Monterchi when you stay at this farm estate. Outbuildings have been carefully converted into rooms and apartments, sleeping 2-6. You can also take the whole property, which accommodates up to 14, or choose B&B (**€**) – with home-made cake and jam for breakfast. The owners are extremely helpful, there's a swimming pool and plenty of lovely country walks.

Casa Pippo, località Lignano, T0575-365555/910251, www.casapippo.it. Immaculate and beautifully furnished, this traditional stone house (closed during 2013) is set in the countryside near Arezzo. It's divided into 2 apartments that can be linked: the whole house sleeps 8, or 10 using a sofa bed, and the small apartment is suitable for 2. There's a heated swimming pool and a gym, and the friendly owners take great care of you. It's a good base for riding and walking. Overnight stays (**€€**) are possible in the low season.

Podere La Foce, Monterchi, T+44(0)7989-864976, www.lafoce.co.uk. May-Oct. A recently renovated 18th-century farmhouse sleeping up to 11 and set in 15 ha of land overlooking Monterchi, La Foce has 3 double bedrooms and a twin (with space for a cot) in the house, and another double bedroom in the converted barn. All bedrooms have en suite marble bathrooms, traditional terracotta floors and chestnut-beamed ceilings. There's a well-equipped kitchen, a dining room and terrace, and a swimming pool in the garden. Weekly lets are usual however shorter stays and out-of-season lets are possible on request.

Il Trebbio, località Ossaia 24, T0575-67002, www.villailtrebbio.it. This 17th-century farmhouse is divided into 3 apartments sleeping 4-6 people. It can also be rented as a whole. The apartments have plenty of character, with rustic beamed ceilings, tiled floors and original fireplaces. Il Trebbio has a swimming pool and well-tended grounds in which to relax, as well as a tiny chapel.

Cortona *p99*
€€€€ **Il Falconiere**, località San Martino 370, T0575-612679, www.ilfalconiere.it. Just a few kilometres outside Cortona, this hotel offers peaceful and elegant accommodation. There are 20 rooms, some in the original villa and others in outlying buildings, decorated in grand country-house style with antiques, 4-poster beds and freestanding baths. There's a swimming pool, a restaurant and even a cookery school.

€€€ **Hotel San Michele**, via Guelfa 15, T0575-604348, www.hotelsanmichele.net. There's plenty of character at this central hotel, which offers good-sized rooms with period features. Suite 214 has a private terrace, and all rooms have a/c. Unusually for Cortona, the hotel also has its own garage, which you can use for an extra charge.

€€€ **Villa Marsili**, viale Cesare Battisti 13, T0575-605252, www.villamarsili.com. On the edge of the old city, this restored 17th-century villa manages to combine elegance and comfort. The cast of *Under the Tuscan Sun* stayed here when filming. Many original features have been preserved, and antiques and Murano glass chandeliers add to the stylish interiors. Most rooms are a good size, and many have lovely views.

€€ **Casa Bellavista**, località Creti, T0575-610311, www.casabellavista.it. At this family-run B&B around 15 km from Cortona you can get a real taste of living the Tuscan dream and enjoy lovely views of the countryside. There are 4 pretty rooms, all furnished in different styles. Breakfast features home-made jams, cakes and fresh cheese and meat – and guests eat together round a large table. Simonetta, the owner, also runs cookery courses, so you can learn how to make your own pasta or Italian bread.

€€ **Casa Chilenne**, via Nazionale 65, T0575-603320, www.casachilenne.com. A steep flight of stairs leads to this light and clean B&B, which opened in 2008 in a medieval building in the heart of Cortona. It's owned by American Jeanette Wong, and there are five rooms, all with freshly tiled bathrooms with refreshingly powerful showers, plasma screen TVs and a/c. There's also a small, light rooftop room, where you can make yourself tea or coffee and relax with a book.

€€ **Relais San Petro in Polvano**, località Polvano 3, Castiglion Fiorentino, T0575-650100, www.polvano.com. Open Mar-Nov. Castiglion Fiorentino is a former Etruscan settlement 12 km north of Cortona, and this lovely hotel is a tastefully converted farmstead in tranquil countryside nearby. The rooms embody rural chic: wooden shutters, tiled floors and wrought-iron bedsteads. You can dine on the terrace on fine days – dishes feature local produce, including the hotel's own olive oil. Take a dip in the pool or wander in the hotel's gardens.

Self-catering
I Pagliai, La Montalla, contact Terretrusche, via Nazionale, 42, Cortona, T575-605287, www.terretrusche.com. This company's properties, dotted around the countryside near Cortona, are reasonably priced and beautifully restored. **I Pagliai** is a converted farm with both apartments and rooms available (the whole property, sleeping 20, can also be rented). Breakfast can be provided on request and there's an old wood-fired pizza oven outside. An apartment for four costs €950 per week; 2-night stays are also possible.

🍴 Restaurants

Arezzo *p94, map p95*
€€€ **Buca di San Francesco**, via San Francesco 1, T0575-23271, www.bucadisan francesco.it. Wed-Sun 1200-1430, 1900-2130, Mon 1200-1430, closed 2 weeks in Jul.

The menu features typical Tuscan fare, including thick *ribollita*, home-made pasta and the local Chianina beef.

€€€ I Tre Bicchieri, piazzetta Sopra i Ponti 3-5, T0575-26557, www.itrebicchieri.it. Mon-Sat and 1st Sun in the month 1200-1400, 1945-2200. Tucked away in a tiny courtyard just off the main shopping street, this restaurant run by brothers Stefano and Leonello has an excellent reputation for the quality of its food and its extensive wine list.

€€€ La Curia, via di Pescaja 6, T0575-333007, www.ristorantelacuria.it. Fri-Tue 1230-1430, 1930-2200, Wed closed. Formal, refined restaurant with gold walls and gilded chairs. Dine in a hushed atmosphere on dishes like pecorino fondue with truffles, porcini risotto, and fillets of Cinta Senese.

€€ Enoteca Bacco and Arianna, via Cesalpino 10, T0575-299598. Daily 1000-1900, Thu-Sat open for dinner till around 2200. This *enoteca* has a frescoed ceiling and old fittings. During the day you come and taste cheeses and wines, while dinner features seasonal food and traditional specialities.

€€ L'Agania, via Mazzini 10, T0575-295381, www.agania.com. Tue-Sun 1200-1500, 1900-2300, open Mon in Aug. Red and white tablecloths and walls give this trattoria a vibrant look. It serves hard-to-find Tuscan dishes and cuts of meat like pigs' trotters and veal cheeks, as well as rabbit, duck and boar.

€ Gastronomia Il Cervo, via Cavour 38/40 on corner of Piazza San Francesco, T0575-20872. Tue-Fri 0730-1500, 1700-2100, Sat 0730-2300, Sun 1000-1500, 1730-2000. Whether you want provisions for a picnic or an informal meal, you'll find it here. Choose what you want from the shop downstairs, then take it away or eat upstairs in the little dining area. Portions are large and fresh.

€ Il Cantuccio, via Madonna del Prato 76, T0575 26830, www.il-cantuccio.it. Thu-Tue 1200-1430, 1900-2230, closed Wed. Cosy dining at this cellar restaurant. Service is swift and friendly, the pasta is home-made and you can choose from a selection of pasta sauces.

€ O Scugnizzo, via Redi 9. Tue-Sun 1930-2330. "Only beer and pizza, is that okay?" says the waitress in this busy pizzeria. And it is when it's this good. The beer menu offers around 180 beers, including Trappist beers from Belgium, and there's plenty of choice of pizza toppings. As well as standard-size pizzas they also serve them 1 m wide – to share of course.

Cafés and bars

Caffè dei Costanti, piazza San Francesco 19, T0575-1824075, www.caffedeicostanti.it. Daily 1930-2400 or later. The walls of this historic café are lined with mirrors. As well as locals drinking espressos at the bar, you'll also find lots of tourists, as the café featured in the film *Life is Beautiful*.

Coffee o'Clock, corso Italia 184, T0575-333067, www.coffeeoclock.com. Daily 0800-2000. Refreshing contemporary café with stripped floors, shiny counters and a large table strewn with papers and magazines. It serves snacks at lunchtime and has Wi-Fi access at €3 per hr.

Fiaschetteria de'Redi, via de' Redi 10, T0575-355012. Tue-Sun 1200-1500, 1930-2230. A lively wine bar that also offers dishes such as bruschetta and salads. Good for a light lunch.

Il Gelato, via Madonna del Prato, on the corner by via di Tolletta. Thu-Mon 1100-2400, shorter hours in winter. A good choice of ice creams at this back-street *gelateria*.

Paradiso, piazza Guido Monaco, T0575-27048. Apr-Oct daily 1200-2330, more erratic in winter. A *gelateria* serving some of the best ices in town.

Monterchi *p98*

€€ La Locanda al Castello di Sorci, Anghiari, 2 km from Monterchi, T0575-789066, www.castellodisorci.it. Closed Mon. This restaurant is set in the grounds of a medieval castle, and is a good place to stop if you're on the Piero della Francesca trail.

It has a relaxed atmosphere and on Sun you're likely to find Italian families enjoying lunch. The pasta is all home-made and the menu changes daily: gnocchi, polenta and *ribollita* could feature.

Cortona *p99*

€€€ Hosteria La Bucaccia, via Ghibellina 17, T0575-606039, www.labucaccia.it. Apr-Nov daily, lunch from 1230, dinner from 1930, closed Mon. Thick stone walls, old wine barrels and plenty of character at this friendly family restaurant on a steep street in Cortona. There's an excellent selection of pecorino cheeses aged from 15 to 180 days, as well as tasty crostini and home-made pasta served with seasonal produce such as truffles or porcini.

€€ La Locanda nel Loggiato, piazza di Pescheria 3, T0575 630575, www.locanda nelloggiato.it. Thu-Tue 1230-1500, 1930-2300. A picturesque setting in the centre of Cortona makes this a favourite place for tourists to eat. You can dine inside or sit out under the romantic loggia. The menu's imaginative, with options like spelt with chicory and Parmesan and Valdichiana steak with pepper and rosemary. In late autumn you might find polenta with white truffle cream.

€€ Osteria del Teatro, via Maffei 2, T0575-630556, www.osteria-del-teatro.it. Thu-Tue 1230-1430, 1930-2130, closed Wed. A historic building, intimate dining areas and walls hung with photos of old theatrical productions make this one of the loveliest places to eat in town. Locals come for special occasions. The food is Tuscan with an imaginative twist, so you might find ravioli filled with pumpkin flowers or beef with lardo di Colonnata and plum sauce. There's an extensive wine list and a good choice of vegetarian dishes. Booking recommended.

€ Croce del Travaglio, via Dardano 1, T0575-62832. Fri-Wed, 1200-1430, 1915-2200. Locals reckon the pizzas here are some of the best in town. They're certainly good value, starting at €4.50. You can dine in the courtyard on fine days.

€ Trattoria Dardano, via Dardano 24, T0575-601944, www.trattoriadardano.com. Thu-Tue 1200-1500, 1900-2200, open daily Jul-Aug. With plain whitewashed walls hung with family photographs, there's a relaxed feel to this simple, busy eatery. The menu consists of uncomplicated Italian and Tuscan dishes – with many of the ingredients produced on the family's farm.

Cafés and bars

Caffè degli Artisti, via Nazionale 18, T0575-601237. Daily 0730-2300, closed Thu Oct-Mar. Central bar/café attracting everyone from locals to tourists who come in for cocktails, Chianti and glasses of beer.

Gelateria Snoopy, piazza Signorelli 29, T0575-630197. Daily 1000-2400, closed Nov-Jan/Feb. Fabulous creamy ices close to Cortona's cathedral. You can have a cone with 4 flavours for under €2 and eat it on a seat outside. Try the fresh strawberry, refreshing peach and orange or the rich crème caramel.

Taverna Pane e Vino, piazza Signorelli 27, T0575-631010, www.pane-vino.it. Tue-Sun 1200-1400, 1900-2300. There are over 900 wines to choose from at this relaxed taverna off the main piazza. You can buy wine by the glass from €2.50, perhaps accompanied by local cheese or bruschetta.

Tuscher, via Nazionale 43, T0575-62053, www.caffetuschercortona.com. Tue-Sun 0800-2100, daily till 2400 in summer (food 1200-1500 only). A lovely café in a historic building, furnished in restrained, contemporary style. Pop in for delicious fresh pasta or bruschetta for lunch. They also serve cocktails and wine by the glass and there's often live music.

⏣ Entertainment

Arezzo *p94, map p95*
Clubs

La Vispa Teresa, www.lavispateresa.it. Outside Arezzo, exit Valdichiana off A1, marked Bettolle (SI). Slick bar and club. Check the website for special dance nights.

Le Mirage Disco, viale di Santa Maria delle Vertighe 34, Monte San Savino, T0575-810215, www.lemirage.it. South of Arezzo, just off A1, take Monte San Savino exit. Various dance anthems and some live music.

Music and theatre
Teatro Comunale Pietro Aretino, via della Bicchieraia 32, T0575-302258/377503. Music, plays and theatre.
Teatro Petrarca, via Guido Monaco 10, T0575-23975. This theatre was closed at the time of writing. It usually stages classical and jazz concerts.

Cortona *p99*
Music and theatre
Teatro Signorelli, piazza Signorelli, T0575-601882, www.teatrosignorelli.com. Wide variety of music, opera, dance, theatre and cinema.

O Shopping

Arezzo *p94, map p95*
Art and antiques
Fiera Antiquaria (Antiques Fair), T0575-377993, www.arezzofieraantiquaria.com. This takes place on the 1st Sun of every month and the preceding Sat. It's a huge event with more than 500 exhibitors spread throughout the streets and squares of Arezzo. It seems to attract everyone from far around.

Clothes and textiles
Busatti, corso Italia 48, T0575-355295, www.busatti.com. Tue-Sat 0900-1300, 1530-1930, Mon 1530-1930. Lovely hand-woven linens – locals come here to stock up on sheets, tablecloths and napkins. You can also visit their workshop out of town at Anghiari (via Mazzini 14, T0575-788013/788424).
Vintage Shed, via San Lorentino 63, T329-323 9035. Mon-Sat 1000-1300, 1800-2000. Tucked away near Porta San Lorentino, this men's clothes shop is crammed with vintage clothes and accessories.

Designer outlets
Dolce e Gabbana, località Santa Maria Maddalena 49, Plan dell'Isola Rignano sull'Arno, T055-833 1300. Mon-Sat 0900-1900, Sun 1500-1900. By train, the nearest station is Rignano sull'Arno.
Prada (Space), località Levanella, Montevarchi, T055-91901/055-919 6528. Mon-Sat 0930-1900, Sun 1000-1300, 1400-2000 (hours subject to change). The nearest station is Montevarchi.
Pratesi, via Dante Alighieri 83, Ambra, www.shoes-pratesi.com. Feb-Oct Mon-Sat 0900-1930, Nov-early Jan Mon-Sat 0900-1230, 1530-1900, closed Jan-end Feb. 30 mins' drive west of Arezzo.

Food and drink
Canto de' Bacci, corso Italia 65, T0575-355804, www.cantodebacci.com. Daily 0800-2000. This *salumeria* stocks all sorts of Tuscan specialities to take home, as well as cheeses, olives, sandwiches and salamis if you want to put together a picnic.
Enoteca Bacco and Arianna, via Cesalpino 10, T0575-299598. Daily 1000-2000. There are 900 different wines for sale here. They'll show you the cellars if you wish, and you can taste Tuscan wines by the glass.

Shoes
The Mall, via Europa 8, Leccio Reggello, T055-865 7775. Mon-Sun 1000-1900. By public transport, train from Arezzo to Montevarchi, then a taxi. Outlet shops here include Gucci, Armani, Ferragamo, Yves St Laurent and Fendi.
Valdichiana Outlet Village, località Le Farniole, Foiano della Chiana, T0575-649926, www.valdichianaoutlet.it. Daily 1000-2000. Off A1 at Valdichiana exit, signs to Foiano della Chiana. Less upmarket (and more affordable) than other retail outlets, this mall houses around 200 discount stores including Nike, Stefanel, Calvin Klein and Sergio Tacchini.

⚙ What to do

Eastern Tuscany *p93*
Cycling and walking
Parco Nazionale delle Foreste Casentinesi, www.parcoforestecasentinesi.it.
The Casentino Forest is in the northern part of Arezzo province, north of Poppi, and stretches into Emilia-Romagna. The national park encompasses woodlands where wolves and wild boar roam. It's great for walkers, as there's a maze of paths to follow, varying from lengthy 'excursions' to nature trails that are more suited to families. There are also mountain bike trails. Visitor centres focus on different aspects of the park: the one at **Badia Prataglia**, via Nazionale 14a, T0575-559477, open all year) concentrates on the relationship between man and the forest. Other centres include **Premilcuore**, via Roma 34, T0543-956540, which is just over the border into Emilia and focuses on the park's wildlife; and **Castagno d'Andrea**, via della Rota 8, T055-837 5125, which looks at the story of Monte Falterona.

⊖ Transport

Arezzo *p94, map p95*
Regular train service to **Florence** (journey 40-60 mins); less frequent service to **Camucia** (nearest station to Cortona, 25 mins), where you can pick up a bus into the town (or a taxi if the bus is late). Terentola is Cortona's other railway station, a bit further from town.

Buses run direct to **Siena** (approx 1 hr 30 mins), **Cortona** (1 hr) and **Sansepolcro** (1 hr). A few buses stop in **Monterchi** (30 mins).

Cortona *p99*
Regular train service from Camucia to **Florence** (1 hr 15 mins), and **Arezzo** (as above).

⊙ Directory

Arezzo *p94, map p95*
Hospital Ospedale San Donato, viale Alcide de Gasperi 17/via Pietro Nenni, T0575-2551. **Pharmacies** Farmacia Centrale, corso Italia 120. Farmacia Merelli, corso Italia 157.

Contents

Footnotes

Index

Titles available in the Footprint *Focus* range

Latin America	UK RRP	US RRP
Bahia & Salvador	£7.99	$11.95
Brazilian Amazon	£7.99	$11.95
Brazilian Pantanal	£6.99	$9.95
Buenos Aires & Pampas	£7.99	$11.95
Cartagena & Caribbean Coast	£7.99	$11.95
Costa Rica	£8.99	$12.95
Cuzco, La Paz & Lake Titicaca	£8.99	$12.95
El Salvador	£5.99	$8.95
Guadalajara & Pacific Coast	£6.99	$9.95
Guatemala	£8.99	$12.95
Guyana, Guyane & Suriname	£5.99	$8.95
Havana	£6.99	$9.95
Honduras	£7.99	$11.95
Nicaragua	£7.99	$11.95
Northeast Argentina & Uruguay	£8.99	$12.95
Paraguay	£5.99	$8.95
Quito & Galápagos Islands	£7.99	$11.95
Recife & Northeast Brazil	£7.99	$11.95
Rio de Janeiro	£8.99	$12.95
São Paulo	£5.99	$8.95
Uruguay	£6.99	$9.95
Venezuela	£8.99	$12.95
Yucatán Peninsula	£6.99	$9.95

Asia	UK RRP	US RRP
Angkor Wat	£5.99	$8.95
Bali & Lombok	£8.99	$12.95
Chennai & Tamil Nadu	£8.99	$12.95
Chiang Mai & Northern Thailand	£7.99	$11.95
Goa	£6.99	$9.95
Gulf of Thailand	£8.99	$12.95
Hanoi & Northern Vietnam	£8.99	$12.95
Ho Chi Minh City & Mekong Delta	£7.99	$11.95
Java	£7.99	$11.95
Kerala	£7.99	$11.95
Kolkata & West Bengal	£5.99	$8.95
Mumbai & Gujarat	£8.99	$12.95

For the latest books, e-books and a wealth of travel information, visit us at:
www.footprinttravelguides.com.

Africa & Middle East	UK RRP	US RRP
Beirut	£6.99	$9.95
Cairo & Nile Delta	£8.99	$12.95
Damascus	£5.99	$8.95
Durban & KwaZulu Natal	£8.99	$12.95
Fès & Northern Morocco	£8.99	$12.95
Jerusalem	£8.99	$12.95
Johannesburg & Kruger National Park	£7.99	$11.95
Kenya's Beaches	£8.99	$12.95
Kilimanjaro & Northern Tanzania	£8.99	$12.95
Luxor to Aswan	£8.99	$12.95
Nairobi & Rift Valley	£7.99	$11.95
Red Sea & Sinai	£7.99	$11.95
Zanzibar & Pemba	£7.99	$11.95

Europe	UK RRP	US RRP
Bilbao & Basque Region	£6.99	$9.95
Brittany West Coast	£7.99	$11.95
Cádiz & Costa de la Luz	£6.99	$9.95
Granada & Sierra Nevada	£6.99	$9.95
Languedoc: Carcassonne to Montpellier	£7.99	$11.95
Málaga	£5.99	$8.95
Marseille & Western Provence	£7.99	$11.95
Orkney & Shetland Islands	£5.99	$8.95
Santander & Picos de Europa	£7.99	$11.95
Sardinia: Alghero & the North	£7.99	$11.95
Sardinia: Cagliari & the South	£7.99	$11.95
Seville	£5.99	$8.95
Sicily: Palermo & the Northwest	£7.99	$11.95
Sicily: Catania & the Southeast	£7.99	$11.95
Siena & Southern Tuscany	£7.99	$11.95
Sorrento, Capri & Amalfi Coast	£6.99	$9.95
Skye & Outer Hebrides	£6.99	$9.95
Verona & Lake Garda	£7.99	$11.95

North America	UK RRP	US RRP
Vancouver & Rockies	£8.99	$12.95

Australasia	UK RRP	US RRP
Brisbane & Queensland	£8.99	$12.95
Perth	£7.99	$11.95

Join us on facebook for the latest travel news, product releases, offers and amazing competitions:
www.facebook.com/footprintbooks.